For Today

For Today

*A Prayer
When Life Gets Messy*

PATRICK ALLEN

 CASCADE Books • Eugene, Oregon

FOR TODAY
A Prayer When Life Gets Messy

Copyright © 2018 Patrick Allen. All rights reserved. Except for brief quotations in critical publications or reviews, no part of this book may be reproduced in any manner without prior written permission from the publisher. Write: Permissions, Wipf and Stock Publishers, 199 W. 8th Ave., Suite 3, Eugene, OR 97401.

Cascade Books
An Imprint of Wipf and Stock Publishers
199 W. 8th Ave., Suite 3
Eugene, OR 97401

www.wipfandstock.com

PAPERBACK ISBN: 978-1-5326-3197-9
HARDCOVER ISBN: 978-1-5326-3199-3
EBOOK ISBN: 978-1-5326-3198-6

Cataloguing-in-Publication data:

Names: Allen, Patrick, author.

Title: For today : a prayer when life gets messy / Patrick Allen.

Description: Eugene, OR: Cascade Books, 2018 | Includes bibliographical references.

Identifiers: ISBN 978-1-5326-3197-9 (paperback) | ISBN 978-1-5326-3199-3 (hardcover) | ISBN 978-1-5326-3198-6 (ebook)

Subjects: LCSH: Prayer—Christianity.

Classification: BV210.2 .A45 2018 (print) | BV210.2 (ebook)

Manufactured in the U.S.A.   JULY 16, 2018

Scripture quotations taken from The Holy Bible, New International Version NIV Copyright 2011 by Biblica, Inc. Used by Permission. All rights reserved worldwide.

"For Today," a prayer found in *Forward Day by Day*, used by permission. Forward Movement, 412 Sycamore Street, Cincinnati, OH, 45202.

Dedication

When you find yourself in the ditch, asking God for enough strength to make it through another day and get back home by dark, it is comforting to have some dear friends who journey with you. I will always be mindful of the way David, Dirk, and Ken stuck with me through thick and thin, and thankful for their listening ear, encouragement, and friendship, literally being the cup of strength to this suffering soul. This book is dedicated to them.

And I would be remiss if I did not acknowledge the constant love, support, and encouragement I received from my wife, Lori, during the difficulties I experienced that preceded this writing project, and during the actual writing of the book. She read every word of the manuscript and patiently listened to numerous versions of the stories contained herein. She is my partner and my rock. Simply put, this book would not have been written without her.

For me, it all comes down to this:
Life is messy, but God is faithful.

Contents

Preface ix
Introduction: O God! xi

PART I: *In the Ditch*

1: Finding Strength for Today 3
2: Losing Courage before Difficulties 20
3: Proving Recreant to Duties 36
4: Losing Faith in Other People 51
5: Enduring Ingratitude, Treachery, and Meanness 68
6: Minding and Giving Little Stings 84

PART II: *On Down the Road*

7: Keeping a Clean Heart 103
8: Facing Failure with Honesty and Courage 119
9: Seeing Good in All Things 134
10: Receiving a New Vision 150
11: Regaining the Spirit of Joy and Gladness 163
12: Being the Cup of Strength to Suffering Souls 174

Closing Comments 185

Preface

This book is based on a prayer written by Phillips Brooks, perhaps best known today for writing "O Little Town of Bethlehem," one of the most beloved of our Christmas carols. However, in his day, he was regarded as one of the best preachers of his generation, and his sermons are still read today. And so is his prayer, "For Today."

My wife and I first discovered this prayer while on a trip to South Carolina, tracing the ministry of John Wesley. We stopped by a beautiful little Episcopal church, and while inside we saw a small daily devotional booklet, *Forward Day by Day*, published by Forward Movement, the publishing arm of the Episcopal Church. "For Today" was printed on the back of the booklet. I was struck by the urgency and honesty of the prayer, so I left some money in the collection basket and took a booklet with me. We are now regular subscribers to *Forward Day by Day*, and have been so for more than fifteen years. We read or recite this prayer every morning as part of our devotions together. Even though I have prayed this prayer thousands of times, it remains fresh and vital each morning.

And I carry a copy of "For Today" in my meeting calendar and notebook. During especially tough times at work (and there have been more than a few), I opened my notebook and silently prayed this prayer. Sometimes during very tough meetings, more than once. It was a comfort and a challenge to not mind little stings or give them, to see good in all things, and to be a cup of strength to suffering souls—even at times when I was the one who was suffering. This prayer has helped me through many a difficult day.

I asked Forward Movement for permission to use this prayer as the foundation for this book, and I am grateful to them for their permission and indebted to Scott Gunn for his encouragement to do so. I have attempted to take each element from the prayer and fashion it into a chapter, first discussing the idea (for example, seeing good in all things), relating it to Scripture, and offering some practical suggestions for making it a reality in your life. There are also some questions for reflection at the end of each chapter that you can use in your private devotions or as part of a small group. It is my hope that the twelve chapters of this book will be helpful to those of us who are crying out, "Oh, God. Give me strength to live another day! I'm just trying to get through the day and back home by dark." As you will see, even in the toughest of times, we are not alone. When life gets messy, God is right there in the mess with us, working to bring hope and healing and grace for the journey.

At the end of the day, this prayer, "For Today," challenges all of us to work through our own difficulties with God's help, and ultimately become a cup of strength to other suffering souls. If this book, *For Today: A Prayer When Life Gets Messy,* can help us do so, then my labors will not have been in vain.

* * *

One final note—each chapter starts with a story. I do have a reputation for being a storyteller, so you might wonder at some point if the stories you are reading are actually true. I can tell you that many of the stories happened just the way I describe them. A few have been purposely modified or merged together with another story or two to shield someone's identity or to make a certain point without sharing too much personal detail. And in a case or two, I tell the story just the way I remember it, but I must confess that my family, friends, colleagues, even a boss or two, may remember it differently. I have been prone to exaggeration on a time or two. This is no attempt at fraud; rather, it is simply the result of the passing of time, an active imagination, numerous retelling of the stories, and perhaps a faulty memory. In any case, the stories are true (that is, there is much truth for the taking) whether they happened just the way I describe them or not.

Patrick Allen
Newberg, Oregon
June 8, 2017

Introduction: O God!

For Today

O God:
Give me strength to live another day;
Let me not turn coward before its difficulties or prove recreant to its duties;
Let me not lose faith in other people;
Keep me sweet and sound of heart, in spite of ingratitude, treachery, or meanness;
Preserve me from minding little stings or giving them;
Help me to keep my heart clean, and to live so honestly and fearlessly that no outward failure can dishearten me or take away the joy of conscious integrity;
Open wide the eyes of my soul that I may see good in all things;
Grant me this day some new vision of thy truth;
Inspire me with the spirit of joy and gladness;
And make me the cup of strength to suffering souls;
In the name of the strong Deliverer, our only Lord and Savior, Jesus Christ.
—PHILLIPS BROOKS

Life is messy. It either has been, is, or will be. We can count on it. It is a part of life, and becoming a Christian is not an insurance policy against tough or terrible times. I wish it was, but it is clearly not. We are not immune from pain, rejection, disappointment, failure, and loss. Yes, life is messy, and sooner or later we will find ourselves in a mess—or a mess will find us. Count on it.

But we can count on another thing, too—God is faithful. Where is God when we are in a mess? Right there in the mess with us, bringing grace and comfort and healing to our situation, even when it is of our own doing, perhaps even more so when this is true. Yes, life is messy, but God is faithful. We can take that to the bank.

Please understand—I am not saying that our messes are necessarily good, or that we should intentionally go around looking for a mess to wallow in just to see God at work. Surely, God is at work all the time, and I suspect that there is a healthy disdain in the heavenly realm for the messes we find ourselves in or make for ourselves. But I am saying that even in the messes we make, God is there and at work. When there is nothing else to hold on to, we can hold on to that. God is present, and faithful, too.

In this book, I want to share a daily prayer that can be truly life giving when we are in the mess of life. It offers words to consistently pray, and wisdom, hope, and resources for our spiritual journey. Several years ago, I found myself praying this prayer almost every day in earnest. You see, my professional work turned into a painful struggle. After a successful thirty-year career, I found myself in a deep mess. I couldn't please my boss, I couldn't garner the support of my colleagues, and I couldn't build a cohesive team or effectively lead those who reported to me. I had succeeded before in other settings, but no matter how hard I tired, all my efforts seemed to end up in criticism, frustration, and, at times, outright failure. I began to lose confidence in my own abilities, and my sense of calling, too.

For the first time in my career, it was obvious to me that some of my colleagues would be happy to see me hit the highway, and they were not shy about sharing their feelings—even in staff meetings with my boss. In spite of my best efforts, they simply didn't want me on the team. I was constantly under attack, and the endless litany of long and empty meetings was mind numbing. I resented the way I was being treated, and I came to fear that I would be dismissed, something that I had never dreamed could happen to me. Honestly, I didn't want to go to work, so I started out each day by praying, "Oh God, give me strength!" Thankfully, strength did come, in many ways, in unexpected ways.

This morning prayer will help you, too, but I must warn you, this may not be a helpful exercise for the spiritually complacent, for those on spiritual autopilot. If life is "all good" and you have no struggles or concerns, you might consider finding another book. This is not a vacation feel-good read. No, this is for those of us who are praying prayers in earnest, in desperation. It is for folk who are in trouble, in pain, in isolation, in despair, in the ditch—and at one time or another, that's most of us. It is not a prayer for those who feel that they have arrived, but for those of us who are still on the journey, walking wearily on a lonely road with no particular destination in sight. This prayer is for those of us who begin the day by crying out, "O God, give me strength!"

I want you to start the practice of praying this prayer, "For Today," each morning. You will find that it is a centering prayer, one that speaks to the core of your spirit and to your particular situation. And together, we will reflect carefully on each phrase, because it is a teaching prayer, too. My earnest desire is that it will carry you as it has carried me. To begin our journey together, I want to tell a story about Reuben Roberts. We can all identify with some of the challenges and opportunities he faced.

Reuben Roberts

Reuben Roberts lived in the hill country of Tennessee on a small farm about eight miles outside of Erin, the county seat of Houston County, just a mile or so down Tennessee Ridge and a short distance from the Tennessee River. The farm consisted of five eight-acre fields used mostly for growing soy beans and hay, a small creek, a springhouse, two old weatherworn storage buildings, an outhouse, and one hundred sixty acres of old-growth hardwoods up on the hill, mostly walnut, oak, hickory, and ash. He and his large family lived in an old walnut log house built sometime just before the Civil War. They tell about the time that some of Grant's troops occupied the house for a time after the Battle of Fort Donelson over in Dover in 1862. They sat around the fireplace chewing and spitting tobacco, and the juice dripped through the floorboards, landing on Confederate soldiers hiding below. I don't know if that really happened, but it is certainly a good story nonetheless. I bought that old farmhouse in the 1980s from one of Reuben's sons. On quiet winter evenings, I would sit by that same fireplace and imagine the conversations that went on so many years before. If only those old walls could talk . . .

In the Tennessee hills, funerals are something special to behold, and they are a celebration of community when an elder is laid to rest. There isn't much liturgy or pomp and circumstance, mostly stories, a few hymns, and shared remembrances—some good, some funny, mostly true. This was true of Reuben's funeral, too. During the service, a middle-aged man rose to speak. "Reuben Roberts was a good man," he began. "He was not only a good farmer, but a good preacher, too. As a young man, he was a circuit rider, a preacher with a horse and a Bible, filling the pulpit on alternate Sundays in Erin and Dixon. Once while returning from Dixon, he was stopped by an angry posse. It seems that someone had robbed, beaten, and otherwise mistreated a young woman in Dixon, and Reuben fit the general description of the perpetrator. The foreman of the posse led Reuben over to a nearby tree and put a rope around his neck. 'Before we hang you, do you have anything to say?' he asked. 'If so, now is the time to utter your last words.' So, Reuben did. He bowed his head and prayed. He prayed for his family, he prayed for his churches, he prayed for his neighbors, he prayed for himself, and then he prayed for his accusers. When he was through, he raised his head, looked the foreman in the eyes, and told him that he was as ready as he ever would be. The foreman cleared his throat, then turned to the posse and said, 'You'd better cut him down, boys, we've got the wrong man.' So, they did."

The storyteller continued, "I've heard that old story about a hundred times now, and told it more than a few times myself. You see, that foreman was my grandfather, and he never forgot the day he almost hung an innocent man. He always cautioned me to avoid judging a book by its cover. There is no doubt, Reuben Roberts was a good man."

As the middle-aged man sat down, a woman just a bit older stood to her feet. "Yes," she began in a matter-of-fact way, "Reuben Roberts was a good man. And not only was he a good preacher, he was a good neighbor, too. You see, late one bitterly cold winter's night, Reuben could not sleep. He woke up worried about his neighbors down the valley—about three miles away. As much as he tried, he couldn't rest, so he got up, dressed, saddled the horse, and headed off down the dirt road toward the river. Like Abraham, he obeyed and went, although he didn't know exactly where he was going or why. As he approached his neighbor's cabin, he saw a dim, flickering light in the window. When he knocked on the door, a small girl appeared and simply began to cry. You see, her daddy was gone and her mother was desperately ill with the flu, near death. There was no food in the house, and the firewood was almost gone. Reuben brought in some wood and stoked the fire. He told the girl that he would return shortly. He rode back to his farm, got his wife out of bed, and sent her back to the neighbor's cabin with some hot food and comfort. He then set off for the town eight miles in the other direction to fetch the doctor. Of course, the doctor was not excited about heading out into the hills on such a terribly cold night, but Reuben persisted. He mentioned later that he had to part with a butchered hog to get the neighbor some help, but he was glad to do so."

The women looked around at those sitting in the church and said in earnest, "I know this happened because I was the little girl in the cabin that night. Truly, Reuben Roberts was a good man."

Slowly, an even older man stood to speak. Stabilizing himself by leaning on his cane and the back of the pew in front of him, he started in a slow but steady voice, "Reuben Roberts was not only a good man and a good neighbor, which he surely was, he was a generous one, too. You see, Reuben also worked for the county as the Road Commissioner during the depression. In those days that mostly meant supervising the road crew as they graded the roads with a blade pulled by a team of mules. One day as they were grading a back road, Reuben saw a young farmer plowing an adjacent field with a two-horse team. Reuben told the road crew to stop and rest as he climbed over the fence to talk to the farmer. 'I don't know exactly why I am doing this,' he told the young farmer, 'but I feel like I should give you this.' He pulled out a five-dollar bill from his pocket and handed it to the farmer. In those days, that was a lot of money. Tears streamed down the farmer's face as he stared at the money in his hand. 'Thank you so much, sir. I don't know how you knew, but last winter was such a terrible one for us. It was so bad, in fact, that we had to eat our seed corn to survive, and this is enough money to buy the seed we need for planting season. I don't know how I can ever repay you.'" The old man finished by saying, "Yes, I know it sounds beyond belief, but I know it happened because I was the young farmer who received that remarkable gift. Reuben Roberts was a good man, indeed. May he rest in peace."

It was as if the benediction had been pronounced. The locals began to disperse from the church, and I quickly made my way across the parking lot and over to the old farmer who told the story about having no seed corn before he could climb into his pickup and drive off. "That was a miracle!" I blurted out. "Yes," he agreed, "how he knew I was in need of seed for planting and generous enough to part with his money during that terrible depression is a true miracle."

"Oh," I said, "the fact that Reuben was sensitive to God's prompting and generous enough to follow through is certainly a wonderful story, but that's not the miracle that I am talking about. No, the miracle for me is that you were out there plowing your fields when you didn't have any seed to plant, plowing without any guarantee of a crop to harvest in the fall. Now, that's a miracle!"

The old farmer just looked up at me with misty eyes, nodded, and smiled at me as I asked, "What made you go out to the barn and hitch up a team in such circumstances? Why would anyone do that without having any seeds to plant?"

"Well," the old farmer said as he gazed off into the distance, "there are times in life when all you can do is get out of bed and step into the work that calls you—and not think about much else. You go to work where you are with what you've got, and you do what you can. If nothing else, hard work has its own reward."

Yes, indeed.

*　*　*

I think there is something in this story for each of us. For one thing, sometimes you are falsely accused or people see things in you or say things about you that are simply not true. They don't seem to see the good in anything you do. This can be so very hurtful, and many times it comes down to one word against another. You can't prove anything. So, what to do? You pray, O God, help! You pray, O God, please let the truth prevail, but above all else, let my character be clearly evident regardless of the outcome—let my life speak. You try to live in such a way that the foreman will say, "Cut the rope, boys. We've got the wrong person." You pray that your life will speak the truth. Of course, there is no guarantee of success, but it is a prayer that leads to conscience integrity. "For Today" speaks to those of us who walk this road.

Sometimes you are on the other end of the rope. You're the one who has misjudged, misunderstood, misconstrued, misapprehended—or even worse. What then? You pray, "O God, I'm sorry. Give me the strength to step forward and admit my mistakes. Let me not wait, make excuses, or rationalize." You owe it to those you have hurt, and to yourself, to make the matter right as quickly and carefully as possible. To be forthright and honest in situations where you have been wrong takes a rare kind of courage, and a good deal of humility, too. You start by praying daily that you will not lose faith in other people—or in yourself.

Sometimes you feel a nudging or hear a still small voice saying—go check on your neighbor. May you be sensitive to the voice of the Holy

Spirit and obedient to God's direction in your life at such times. When you sense God at work, lean in. But sometimes you are the one in desperate need, often because of your own poor choices. What then? You pray, "O God, help me to be perceptive enough to recognize and humble enough to accept help and assistance when offered. And help me to deal with my own pride and have the courage to ask for help when I am in need." That takes a rare form of courage, too. In the end, you pray that you will be the cup of strength to suffering souls, and trust that others will bear the cup for you in your own time of need.

Sometimes helping a neighbor in need or a stranger in crisis costs more than you anticipate, maybe even a butchered hog. So be it. May you also pray, "O God, help me to hold whatever I have so loosely that it may be freely used to help a neighbor in need, or a Samaritan in a ditch. And help me to see those around me, to pay attention." It is so easy to go about our business as though everyone else was simply put on this earth for our own comfort. We really do need each other, and it begins by intentionally seeing one another and seeing good in all things. O God, may this be our prayer, too.

And sometimes you are faced with an overwhelming challenge without the resources in hand to complete the task. It's time to plant and you have no seed corn. Most of us have been there at one time or another, or are there right now. The temptation is to simply quit and walk away, to give up, or to make excuses or blame others for the difficulties. It is a much more difficult task to keep leaning in, to keep doing what you can where you're at, and using what you've got to work with. That is a prayer by action: "O God, I don't know where the seed will come from, but it is time to plant so I will hitch up the horses. O God, if you are present, then I will persevere." Of course, there are no guarantees that someone will climb over the fence, hand you some money, and solve your immediate problem, but I do believe that there are more resources available to all of us (both material and eternal) than we can possibly imagine. It is a daily prayer for courage to face today's difficulties. As Jesus reminded us, tomorrow will care for itself.

In this book, we will learn to pray a simple daily prayer and meditate on various strategies and outlooks suggested in the prayer for getting through tough days—and on to higher ground. I deeply believe that God wants all of us to prosper and grow, but right now you're in the muck and mire and need to keep moving day by day. So, you pray, "O God, help me to keep my head up and my eyes fixed on you. One day I'll plant a spiritual garden on fertile ground, but right now I need strategies to help me through today, to get out of the ditch."

So, we begin. I trust that you will pray this morning prayer, "For Today," each day, and take time to reflect upon and practice each part of the prayer. This is not a prayer to make anyone an instant saint; it is a prayer when the ox is in the ditch or the seed corn is gone—a prayer when you are just trying to make it through the day in the midst of tough and even terrible times. With God's help, together we will learn to be faithful in the hard times, and look forward to better days ahead. O God, bless our journey together.

Part I

IN THE DITCH

This book is written in two parts: "In the Ditch" (part 1) and "On Down the Road" (part 2). For most of us, we want to focus on getting on down the road, which is certainly normal since that is where we want to be, but first we have to deal with the reality of the ditch. No use trying to ignore it, act like it is not there, rationalize, or explain it away. Before we can head on down the road again, we have to acknowledge and, in fact, embrace the ditch, as distasteful and painful as that may be at times. So, we begin by examining some of the realities and maladies we will face while in the ditch: finding strength for today (chapter 1), losing courage before difficulties (chapter 2), proving recreant to duties (chapter 3), losing faith in other people (chapter 4), enduring ingratitude, treachery, and meanness (chapter 5), and minding little stings—and sometimes giving them (chapter 6).

We will examine each reality in turn before looking at what I call restorative practices that help you get on down the road in part 2: keeping a clean heart (chapter 7), facing failures with honesty and courage (chapter 8), seeing good in all things (chapter 9), and receiving a new vision of God's truth (chapter 10). Ultimately, as the prayer states, we, all of us, want to regain the spirit of joy and gladness (chapter 11) and become the cup of strength to other suffering souls (chapter 12), and we can get there, too. But before we turn our attention to helping others who are in the ditch, we first have to find our way out of the ditch and head on down the road. Along the way, we will learn that ministering to others is a wonderful calling, but we must do so out of the overflow of our spirit—and that takes self-care. So, we begin with this earnest prayer: *Oh, God. Give me strength to live another day!*

1

Finding Strength for Today

> Give us today our daily bread.
> —MATTHEW 6:11

Introduction

There are times, tough times, when all you want to do is get through the day. All you can do is try to get through the day. No planning for the long haul, no finding the color of your parachute, no crafting a personal vision statement, no envisioning a better me, no finding out who hid the cheese, no adding another line to your résumé, no trying to weave a beautiful tapestry out of the tangled strands of your difficulties, and no making lemonade out of lemons. You just hope to find a way to make it through today, this day, and get back home before dark. That's all you have the strength and vision to do.

There are times when you are literally at the end of your rope, burdened by problems and struggles not of your own making. At other times, the difficulties are totally your own doing, the result of silly or selfish or sinful decisions. In either case, you face the day with dwindling hope and no energy to pray. The words just aren't there to accurately express the depth of the weariness, desperation, hurt, and despair you feel. All you can pray is, "Oh, God. Give me strength to live another day." What a wonderfully honest prayer.

In this chapter, we will look carefully at the kind of strength we need to get through the day and some sources and resources for that strength. Then, we will look at two related qualities in chapters 2 and 3—courage and resolve. As we will see, these elements are crucial to recovery but they can easily become lost in the ditch. First, however, let's talk about the strength we need for today.

Give Me Strength

Clearly, some people have more inner strength or resolve or resilience or grit, whatever you want to call it, than others. They just seem to have an inner capacity to keep leaning in when facing difficult and trying times. I guess that some of us just have a broader bandwidth than others for such things, but sooner or later it seems to me that just about all of us hit the wall—or the wall hits us. There comes a point when being stubborn is simply not enough, a failed strategy. Thankfully, I have good news. When you're in the ditch, you are not alone, and you don't have to rely solely on your own strength to make your way. There is such a thing as outer strength, too, and it is a wonderful gift.

Strength Is a Gift

Yes, strength is a gift, and it is one of the most important gifts we can receive. And who is the giver? The Scriptures make this very clear, "It is God who arms me with strength and keeps my way secure" (2 Sam 22:33). Yes, God is the giver of strength. This is the testimony of King David, and if anyone ought to know about receiving strength in the midst of tough times and terrible circumstances (some the result of his own doing), it would be David. This promise is affirmed in Isaiah, who spoke these prophetic words: "So do not fear, for I am with you; do not be dismayed, for I am your God. I will strengthen you and help you; I will uphold you with my righteous right hand" (Isa 41:10). What a wonderful thing it is to hear the voices of experience confirm God's faithfulness in difficult times. We can add the voice of Moses, too, who sang, "The Lord is my strength and my defense" (Exod 15:2a). What a song, and we can sing that song, too!

Of course, singing such a song will take some practice, for as Isaiah reminds us, "Even youths grow tired and weary, and young men stumble and fall" (Isa 40:30). Sounds familiar, doesn't it—growing tired and weary, stumbling, falling? Yes, when you're in the ditch, you grow tired and weary. That's to be expected, but thankfully Isaiah doesn't end there. He doesn't leave us in the ditch without resources or hope. He adds quickly and confidently, "But those who hope in the Lord will renew their strength. They will soar on wings like eagles; they will run and not grow weary, they will walk and not be faint" (Isa 40:31). What a promise—the Lord will renew our strength, and we will someday soar again.

You might well be thinking, however, "This is a wonderful promise, but right now I'm not trying to soar to new heights. I'm just trying to get home before dark!" Fair enough. The important thing to remember here, even and especially in the darkest of times and places, is that you do not, in fact, cannot, do this solely in your own strength. Strength for today is a gift from God. Remember Jesus' words recorded in the Gospel of John, "I am the vine; you are the branches. If you remain in me and I in you, you will bear much fruit" (John 15:5a). What good news it is that God is the vine, and we are the branches. Branches draw their strength from the vine. They are not independent agents. In fact, apart from the vine, branches shrivel quickly and die quietly. The life-giving power is in the vine. Relying solely on our own strength is the best strategy I know to take up permanent residence in the ditch. So, in whatever you do, do it in the strength God provides. And when you do, you will bear much fruit—in season.

Refuge

But let's be honest. Bearing fruit in season with the strength provided by God is a breathtaking promise. Of course, we all look forward to that day, but today we are in the ditch and more interested in refuge than strength. I've been there, too. Having strength to fight the battle sounds good, but right now we just want to be still, curl up in some safe place, listen to some music, close our eyes, and take a long nap.

In ancient times, Hawaiians lived under very strict communal laws. The chief remained disconnected from the commoners, who by sacred law had to keep their distance from the chief. In fact, they could not touch any of his possessions, walk in his footprints, or let their shadows touch any part of the chief's royal properties. Even the slightest infraction could result in an immediate death penalty. The offender would be chased down and executed on the spot—unless, that is, he or she could flee and enter a place of refuge. It was literally a life or death race. Once inside, the offender could be purified and over time restored to the community. It was a time of rest, reflection, and spiritual renewal. I think there are times when we all need a place of refuge like that, maybe even today.

I love the synonyms for refuge: sanctuary, shelter, protection, asylum, safe harbor, hideout, haven, and retreat. When we are in the ditch, we long for a place of refuge and strength, and it is important to keep in mind that you don't have to choose between the two. In fact, they are intrinsically joined one with the other, like two sides of the same coin. The psalmists make this abundantly clear: "The Lord is my strength and my shield" (28:7a); "The Lord is my strength and my defense" (118:14); and "God is our refuge and strength, an ever-present help in trouble" (46:1). You see, God's ever-present help in times of trouble includes both refuge and strength. Now that's a promise to hold on to! It is certainly a comfort to know that "whoever dwells in the shelter of the Most High will rest in the shadow of the Almighty" (91:1). Yes, indeed, when we are in the ditch, rest is necessary but so very difficult to find. As it turns out, rest, like strength, can be a spiritual gift, too.

And there is more good news. Unlike the Hawaiian chiefs, God has not set himself apart from us with punishing, exclusionary rules, or set up some special place of refuge that we need to find and enter for safety while evading our accusers along the way. It is not a life or death race to safety. Rather, it is quite the opposite. Remember the story of the Prodigal Son as told in the Gospel of Luke? The son leaves home, wildly spending his inheritance, and otherwise making a mess of his life before deciding to head for home. According to the parable, "But while he was still a long way off, his father saw him and was filled with compassion for him; he ran to his son, threw his arms around him and kissed him" (15:20). In this story, of course, we, all of us, are the sons and daughters, and God is the father. As it turns out, we don't need to make our way to a place of refuge to find grace because God is coming our way, running to us! Even as we pray a desperate prayer asking for strength for another day, it is so good to know that strength and refuge are already on the way.

Strength in Weakness

Before we move on to examine the second half of the first line of this prayer, "Oh, God. Give me strength *to live another day*," we need to discuss one more aspect about asking God for strength. Yes, we admit that we do not get out of the ditch solely with our own strength. Yes, strength is certainly a gift from God. Yes, there is refuge in times of trouble. And yes, as we turn our hearts toward home, we do not need to find a designated place of refuge because Grace comes running to us. For all of this, we are so very thankful.

Still, while these promises and realities are a comfort, I have to admit that in the still, dark moments in the middle of a long and sleepless night, we can still feel weak, broken, and so very much left to our own wits. Sometimes it helps to be reminded of such Scripture verses as "For when I am weak, then I am strong" (2 Cor 12:10) or "I can do all this through him who gives me strength" (Phil 4:13). Of course, these are true, but when you're in the ditch, in despair, these verses can come across more like a spiritual version of the old bromide "when life gives you lemons, then make lemonade!" than a profound spiritual insight. Sometimes, the last thing we want to hear from someone is, "I'll be praying for you," especially from those who are passing by, too busy or fearful or simply not concerned enough to stop, lean in, and lend a helping hand. They see you in the ditch, but don't want to get their hands dirty. They offer an insincere promise of remembrance and some drive-by spiritual comfort.

There are other verses that seem to me to be more helpful, particularly because the focus is not on "me" and what "I" can do, but rather on what God can do in and through us. For example, "the Spirit helps us in our weakness" (Rom 8:26) and "my grace is sufficient for you, for my power is made perfect in weakness" (2 Cor 12:9). I suppose we are drawn to these verses and others like them because there is a certain comfort for us in times of weakness. We don't have to act like spiritual giants to draw strength from them, and this is good news because the last thing you want to do when you're in the ditch is to put on a superhero's costume and fly off to save the world. You just want to make it through the day, and you'll take all the help you can get.

What makes it so difficult to find strength for many of us is that the church—especially the Sunday morning service—is the last place to find support and solace in times of need. Sadly, in so many of our churches, we are expected to bravely put on a happy face and sing about being "happy, happy, happy all the time," even when we're hurting and broken inside. There are very few praise choruses that allow us to lament. It's as if there is an unwritten rule that we don't bring our difficulties to church. Instead, we are to put on a mask and act as if everything is fine, and we go home discouraged and empty. Sadly, many of us do not go back.

I am convinced that we must embrace our struggles, our pain, our fears, rather than ignore or minimize them. Fierce embrace, I have come to believe, stimulates growth. It is an essential part of the growth process, so our lament needs to find expression. There are no spiritual shortcuts. Embracing our lament and facing our difficulties squarely requires real inner strength. Sometimes the hardest thing to do is to let go of a dream, have a good cry, extend forgiveness, or walk away, knowing that it was not to be. When we ask God for strength for today, we need to be mindful and receptive of this kind of strength, too. Honest lament takes the rawest kind of courage, but it is through lament that we find grace and sustenance and growth. In short, it is how we find our way. I have come to believe that spiritual insight comes more through the difficulties we face and embrace than through the successes we celebrate, allowing us to gain a deeper understanding of what God is doing in our neighborhoods—and in our own lives. Far too often, it is the success stories that are recognized and glorified in our churches and chapels, but if truth be told, we could learn a good deal more about spiritual growth by being bone honest about the failures around us—and in our own lives, too, than by sharing all our victory stories.

I want to close this portion of the chapter devoted to finding strength for today by sharing a very familiar verse from perhaps the best known and most beloved psalm of all time—the 23rd Psalm, "You prepare a table before me in the presence of my enemies" (23:5a). Honestly, when I am in the ditch, in the midst of a battle, I want my enemies to be defeated and publicly humiliated. I am not interested in a cease-fire, but note in this verse that there is no promise that everything will go our way or that our difficulties will just fade away. No, being a Christian is simply not an insurance policy against pain, sickness, betrayal, embarrassment, rejection, or loss. I certainly wish it were, but clearly it is not. And there are no guarantees that God will swoop in like an angry mother hen and chase away all our enemies. I've wished for that type of intervention myself a time or two, but my experience is that that rarely happens.

What King David (the writer of Psalm 23) does affirm from his own spiritual journey is that God will prepare a table for us *in the midst* of our enemies. Think about it—in the middle of the battle, God will set a table for us, a feast, a sanctuary, where we can take nourishment and find grace, inner peace, insight, and comfort. We cry out to God, asking for enough strength for today, and God throws a banquet right where we are, in the midst of our enemies, in the ditch. Is it any wonder that the most quoted lament in Scripture, "My God, my God, why have you forsaken me" (Ps 22:1a), words Jesus quoted from the cross, open the psalm just before Psalm 23? In some profound, spiritually-connected way, Psalm 22 and Psalm 23 knit together, forming a beautiful tapestry. It is from and through lament during times when we are at our worst that we see God's grace at its best—preparing a table for us in the midst of our enemies, even when it turns out that our worst enemy is us.

To Live Another Day

When we pray, "Oh God. Give me strength to live another day," it is important to keep the focus on the right day—today. Not yesterday, filled with shame, guilt, regret, and recrimination; and not tomorrow, filled with anxiety, uncertainty, and a few fantasies, too. Even though we all know that it is unhealthy to live in the past and impossible to live in the future, we still try to do so from time to time. Memories and dreams are often comforting, but they are a fleeting, temporary respite. It will take courage (chapter 2) and resolve (chapter 3) to stay in the moment, but deep down we know that we can't reminisce or wish our way out of the ditch. We have to lean into today. That's really the only day we have to work with.

Daily Bread

When Jesus was asked how we should pray, he made it clear that we are to ask boldly for our daily bread: "Give us *today* our *daily* bread" (Matt 6:11). But why the double emphasis: today and daily? It certainly affirms what we just discussed—we need to focus on *today*, not yesterday and not tomorrow. Give us bread for today, please. Tomorrow will carry its own concerns. Worrying about tomorrow solves nothing and simply puts an added burden on today. When you're in the ditch, the last thing you need is an extra load to carry. Bearing extra weight is simply a hindrance, and particularly so if you are intent on getting out of the ditch and on down the road called life. Any experienced hiker will tell you that it is best to travel as lightly as possible, carrying only what is needed for the journey. Excess baggage complicates everything.

And note that we were not instructed to ask for or expect a month's supply of bread, only enough for today, our *daily* bread. The old Quakers have a saying, "Way will open in front of you, and Way will close behind you." Way unfolds and closes day by day. Investing your energies in trying to see and understand the entire journey at the outset is not possible or helpful. Just put one step in front of the other and keep walking. Way will open. Like manna in the desert, daily bread will be provided. You can count on it. Even when a table is set for you in the midst of the battle, the serving is for today. No doggy bags. Tomorrow will care for itself. This prayer is an extension of our faith in God's character and ability to provide for this day—give us today our daily bread.

Of course, the temptation is to feast on emotional candy instead of daily bread. Candy is sweet and provides a bit of instant energy, but it does not provide the nutrients that will sustain you in times of crisis. Let me name three sweets to avoid: denial, avoidance, and wishful thinking. Rather than the hard work of lament and asking for daily bread, those in denial choose to act as if there is nothing wrong, saying in one way or another, "I'm not hungry and the cupboard is full, so there's really no need to ask for daily bread. I've got it all under control." In the very short run, it is a way to cope and get through the moment. However, it is simply a subtle form of self-deception. At the end of the day, those in denial will find that they are still in the ditch—hungry, malnourished, and disillusioned, too.

Another sweet treat to sidestep is avoidance. We, all of us, can be procrastinators at times, and some of us have it down to an exact science. If it is in the least bit unpleasant, we put it at the bottom of the to-do list. One of the first strategies taught in time management seminars is to move the important things to the top of the to-do list and get them done first, and don't put off the unpleasant tasks till the end of the day. When we do, more times than not, they will be done poorly or not get done at all. When in the ditch, it is so overwhelming to enter into difficult conversations, ask for help, or even appear in public. Yet, these are precisely the things we need to do to move on. In effect, they're part of our daily bread. As our parents insisted when we were children, we need to eat our vegetables even though we would much rather have dessert. I think God is, in effect, saying the same thing. We pay a price for denial and avoidance.

The third tempting sweet is wishful thinking. A great deal of emotional energy can be expended on efforts to create an alternate reality, wishing for what we would like to see instead of an honest lament about what actually is. Along with denial and avoidance, wishful thinking is a delay tactic, but what is actually being delayed is our own growth and recovery. It's much better to chew on reality and squarely face the difficulties, especially if they are the result of our own shortcomings, mistakes, even sin.

When we ask God to give us strength to live another day, we need to be open to all that that gift entails. Far too often, our understanding of strength is limited to having physical energy, but there is much more. Wouldn't it be helpful to think about strength in a plural—strengths? In addition to physical strength, we can pray that we will display the attributes of strength such as tenacity, soundness, and mental stamina. And we can pray for the abilities that strength provides: insight, resourcefulness, understanding, competence, knack, and savvy. Jesus instructed all of us to ask for our daily bread. I have no doubt that it will arrive on schedule, and it will provide strength(s) for body, mind, and spirit.

I think it is important to note that Jesus instructed us to ask for *our* daily bread, not *my* daily bread. In fact, in the Lord's Prayer, there is not one *me* or *my*, it is always *us* and *our*. Jesus made it very clear that the matter of receiving daily bread is a communal act. In a profoundly spiritual sense, when someone is hungry, we are all diminished—and hungry, too. Perhaps that is why Jesus insisted that the second great commandment for all of us is to love our neighbors as we love ourselves (Matt 22:39). After all, we are all in need of daily bread in one form or another.

Not by Bread Alone

Clearly, we are to ask God for our daily bread, but that does not mean that we are to live by bread alone. That would be a mistake. When we find ourselves in the ditch, it can be so very lonely, almost as if we are invisible. And with such feelings, it is easy to withdraw and insulate, even hide. Yet, it is precisely when we are in the ditch that we need others the most, especially models, directors, and even a Sherpa or two.

For ten years, I had the privilege of working for a university with a seaside campus in San Diego. I had a magnificent ocean view from my office. Every year I looked forward to watching the whale migrations that took place in December and January right outside my window. They were spectacular events. It was not unusual to spot twenty or thirty whales in a single afternoon, yet I knew students who spent four years on campus and never spotted a single whale. Not even one! How could this be? The simple answer beyond an overwhelming preoccupation with social media is that they didn't know what they were looking for, and the Pacific Ocean is simply too expansive for a casual glance every now and then in search of a whale. You don't find whales that way.

I was often asked for advice about how to spot whales, and I was always happy to oblige. "All you have to do," I would say, "is watch for the whale boats. They will lead you right to the whales. From our campus vantage point, you can see the whale-watching boats head out of the San Diego harbor and up the coast. When they detect a pod of whales, they will turn around and follow about one hundred yards behind them. Just look in front of the boat and you will see some whale spouts. Keep looking. Next, you will see their backs and flukes as they break the surface of the water and slowly begin a deep dive. It's that simple. If you want to see some whales, watch the whale boats."

It is easy to lose our sight lines, our perspective, when we're in the ditch. Life just looks differently from that angle, usually darker and more sinister, so it is important to have some whale boats in our lives; some wise friends who can point the way forward, model appropriate behavior, ask tough questions, and keep us grounded in reality. The last thing we need when we're in the ditch is to lose our sense of true north. When that happens, we tend to struggle and flail in the ditch rather than take concrete steps to get out of it. At the end of the day, we are exhausted from the journey of a few feet, but still in the same ditch.

A Sherpa can be of great help, too. If you are inclined to climb a high and treacherous mountain, it is good to have a guide who has been there before. Someone who knows the right places to rest, the safest places to camp, the weather, and the best routes to the top and back down the mountain. Someone who in tough times can carry part of your load, and if needed, offer first aid. When you begin to describe your struggles and fears, a Sherpa will look you squarely in the eyes and say, "Me, too. I've been there. Walk with me."

I must admit that it can be difficult to find a Sherpa, particularly so if we are isolated or in denial, and it is even harder to summon the courage to ask for help when we find one, but with effort we can identify those who have walked in our shoes. Most "me, too" people are happy to walk and talk with you as you struggle to get out of the ditch. After all, they were in the ditch, too.

Sherpas can guide us because of their experience; they've been where we are heading and they know what difficulties we will encounter along the way. Mentors and directors can orient us because they have wisdom; they know the right questions to ask and how and when to speak into our lives. This is one of the rarest gifts, a treasure, someone who sees the best in us and asks for our best, too. Someone who pushes us to maintain a proper perspective, live in reality, and do the right things. They also help us contemplate the spiritual dimensions of our situation to see how God is at work in times of difficulty, and to hear what God may be saying to us or asking of us in the midst of them. Such support is truly grace at work.

Sherpas, mentors, and directors are the wisdom keepers in our lives. They keep us focused on the things that are important. Proverbs reminds all of us that "the wise listen to advice" (12:15) and "plans are established by seeking advice" (20:18). A "ditch experience" can indeed be humbling, but it often makes us receptive to the advice of those around us. At such vulnerable times, it is so very important to be careful and selective about who we allow to speak into our lives. Look for those who have wisdom and experience. Look for the "me, too," not the "well, if I were you" people. If you want to see the whales, look for the whale boats.

Scripture

I am a bit hesitant about including a section like this in each chapter, not because I do not see the wisdom contained in Scripture, but because it is so very easy to quote a verse or two and extrapolate meanings from them to prove one's own point of view—a practice called proof texting. I've heard it done in many a Sunday sermon over the years, and I've done it myself on an occasion or two. Yet the stories in the Bible are our stories, too, and they do speak to all of us in deep and significant ways. For that reason, I include this section and pledge to be as fair and faithful to the text as I know how to be.

Guiding Pillars

When we find ourselves in trouble, in the ditch, it is easy to lose sight of God in the mess, to not recognize his presence. We ask, "Where is God? Have I been abandoned?" It is an honest response and fair questions to ask. Exodus, the second book in the Old Testament, tells the story of the

Israelites' journey out of slavery in Egypt and into the wilderness, heading for the promised land. As they went, they were led by a pillar of cloud by day and a pillar of fire by night. Assuredly, "Neither the pillar of cloud by day nor the pillar of fire by night left its place in front of the people" (Exod 13:22). It must have given great comfort and confidence to the people of Israel to know that God was leading them, and to have tangible, visible evidence in front of them at all times.

But when Pharaoh's army approached the Israelites from behind, the Israelites were literally caught between the devil and the deep blue sea. And to make matters worse, the pillar of cloud and the pillar of fire began to move; they "withdrew and went behind them" (14:19). Can't you imagine the fear that struck deep in the hearts of the Israelites? Just when they found themselves in a deep and dangerous ditch, God moved to the rear, out of sight!

Of course, there is the rest of the story. The pillar of fire continued to give light to the Israelites so they could work throughout the night, and the pillar of cloud brought an unusually dark night to the Egyptian army. They stayed in their camp and did not advance, and when they did the next morning, it was a total disaster. All in all, it is fair to say that God had their backs, whether the Israelites knew it or not. God was there all the time, in the mess, working in unexpected and unimaginable ways.

In a profoundly real way, the exodus story is our story, too. We all pray and look for God's presence and guidance as we journey out of slavery of one kind or another. Sometimes, however, we end up in the ditch and God is nowhere to be seen or heard. On such occasions, it is a very human response to ask, "Where is God? Have I been abandoned?" The simple answer is no; you have not been abandoned. And where is God when you can't see his handiwork or feel his presence? God is still right there in the mess with you, and you can be confident that he has your back, bringing grace, healing, and goodness to whatever you are facing, even when what you are facing is horrible. Remember, he will set a table for you in the midst of your enemies. And he is at the table, too, urging you to come and dine.

Some Practical Advice

Before ending this chapter with some questions for reflection and discussion, I want to offer some practical advice when we face tough times. In some respects, they are quite simple, but they are not simplistic. If taken to heart and put into practice, I truly believe that they will help us make it through the day. I know that they have helped me make it through some dark days, and through some very dark nights, too. Even while we pray to God for strength to meet the trials of the day, strength we do not have, there are some concrete things we can do to partner with God and ease the way. As the old Russian proverb tells us, trust in God but row toward shore.

Bookend Your Day

By bookending your day, I simply mean to start and finish your day with a routine, a time of resolve and reflection. Start out each day with fifteen minutes of quiet time, looking to what awaits you, asking God for strength and guidance, and listening for his voice. And it may seem a bit hokey, but many find it helpful to focus their thoughts by lighting a candle, signifying that God's spirit is present. (Of course, you don't have to light a candle to have God with you, but it is a tangible symbol and reminder of his presence.) Then, read out loud "For Today," the prayer that is the focus of this book. Memorize it. Let it speak to you. Then be still. Let God speak to you. I have come to believe that we spend far too much time in prayer talking rather than listening. Just say, "Speak Lord, I am listening," and then really listen. Begin each day with resolve—asking, listening, and gathering strength for the day.

And end your day in gratitude. Just before you turn out the lights, light a candle and take fifteen minutes to reflect on the times when you felt closest to God during the day, and on what things and relationships brought you joy and gave you energy. Be thankful for those small rays of hope and renewal that came even in the midst of your darkest days. So, bookend your day; make it a practice to start each day with hope and end each day with gratitude. If you do, it will slowly but surely change you in surprising ways.

Find Your Thin Places

Thin places are those places or events in life where the dividing line between the holy and the ordinary is very thin . . . to the point that the ordinary becomes holy and the holy becomes ordinary. Honestly, I believe that the distinction between the sacred and the secular can be confusing, and at times, unnecessary. Still, I must admit that there are thin places in my life, places and events where I feel very close to God. If you are in the ditch, my advice is to seek out your thin places as often as possible. For me, the redwoods and the ocean are thin places. They calm my spirit, give me courage, and renew my strength. I try to visit them on a regular basis.

There are also thin places that are not as dramatic or awe inspiring as a redwood grove in Northern California or a walk along the Oregon coast. It is possible to find thin places in your daily routine, too. In fact, I urge you to do so. Earlier in this chapter, I told about a time when I was facing painful difficulties in my job. It was a chore to just show up for work most days. At lunch, my wife would swing by and pick me up. We would grab a sandwich and then go for a twenty-minute drive in the country. Those little daily rides were truly life-giving, thin places that carried me through the rest of some very dreadful days. They saved my spirit.

Live with Hope

There's an old Appalachian saying: "Hope for the best, prepare for the worst, and be grateful for whatever comes." I like that very much. Even while we do our best to be prepared for the worst eventuality, we can choose to face each day with hope and gratitude. It is our choice. We don't deny the darkness, but we choose to live in the light because we know that even a small amount of light can expel a great deal of darkness. We simply and faithfully focus on the light. Clearly, hopefulness is a choice we can embrace or reject. In difficult circumstances, there is often very little over which we have control, but optimism is one of them. It is our choice.

Perhaps a more difficult spiritual practice is to be grateful for whatever comes. Honestly, I do not always know how to think about the circumstances I face. Are they the will of God, the work of the Evil One, the consequences of my own actions, random events, or a combination of these factors—or something else altogether? I really do not know. But I do know that in facing whatever events come my way, I have the choice to either blame and complain or to be thankful and look for what I can learn from the situation. I readily admit that such a tact is not easy and it may come across as silly, but I truly believe that it is not. Even in the darkest of times, we who believe in the goodness and grace of God draw strength not from what we face, but from the character and promises of the God who is with us in our difficulties, who sets a feast for us in the midst of our enemies. We hope for the best and express gratitude for whatever comes as an act of faith and trust in the one who hears and answers this earnest pray, *Oh God. Give me strength to live another day!*

Don't Get Stuck in the Mud

One final word of advice: don't get stuck in the mud. Don't wallow in self-pity or blame, or allow a sense of helplessness to sink in. Focus on what you can do, not on what you can't do. Focus on today, not on what happened yesterday or what might happen tomorrow. Like the young farmer in the Reuben Roberts story, hitch up the horses and lean into the task or trial that is before you. Do what you can and keep moving.

And remember that getting through the day and out of the ditch is a team sport, not a marathon—even if at times it feels that way. Don't go it alone. The best strategy, it seems to me, is to rely on God's gifts and promises, the wisdom and support of others, and your own best efforts. Give others a chance to come alongside and help, as uncomfortable and embarrassing as it might feel to do so at the time.

Finally, make a copy of this prayer, "For Today," and carry it with you. Memorize it, too. I have a copy of this prayer tucked inside the front flap of the notebook that I carry to every meeting I attend. During difficult times when I felt under attack, unappreciated, or unduly criticized, I would open my notebook and read this prayer—sometimes three of four times in a single meeting. And now when I open my notebook at the start of a very good meeting, it serves as a reminder that God was, is, and will be faithful, giving strength for today.

Conclusion

In this chapter, we looked carefully at the first line of a prayer "For Today," by Phillips Brooks: "Oh God. Give me strength to live another day." It is a prayer prayed in desperation, in times when we're in the ditch. We noted that strength for today can be a gift from God; we don't have to depend solely on our own strength. And we saw in Scripture that gaining strength and finding refuge are closely related. In fact, God comes running to us in our time of need. In addition, there is strength to be had in our weakest moments, and God prepares a table for us *in the midst* of our enemies.

Next, we examined what it means to ask for our daily bread, not *my* but *our* daily bread, and the problems that result when we feast on denial, avoidance, and wishful thinking instead. And there are guides (Sherpas), mentors, and wise friends who will walk with us in our most difficult days. As it turns out, getting out of the ditch is a team sport, not a marathon. Even though in times of crisis our instincts are to hide, there is strength in community and fellowship.

In Scripture, we looked at the story of the Israelites' exodus from bondage in Egypt, and noted that it is our story, too. Sometimes when it is difficult to see or hear anything, God is at work nonetheless, serving as light and protection in our darkest nights. As one of my mentors loved to say, even when you think nothing is happening, something is happening.

And finally, several words of practical advice were offered: bookend your day, visit your thin places, live with hope, and don't get stuck in the mud. In our loneliest hours, when the pain and difficulties seem insurmountable, all we know to do is cry out and pray, "Oh God, give me strength to live another day." In doing so, we place our confidence and trust in the character and promises of God, resources that are beyond our imagination, and we connect to a reality that is beyond our comprehension.

Questions for Reflection and Discussion

1. Why is it so difficult in times of need to ask for help? Is it pride, embarrassment, shame, or something else?

2. Why do we hide and otherwise isolate ourselves in difficult times, times when we so much need the care, fellowship, and support from others?

3. What are the thin places in your life? Do you visit them regularly? How do they renew your spirit?

4. Do you have Sherpas, mentors, and wise friends who will journey with you? If so, how have they walked with you, and if not, where might you find them?

5. Do you bookend your day? If not, how might you go about the spiritual practice of intentionally starting your day with hope and ending your day with gratitude?

FOR TODAY

Oh, God:
Give me strength to live another day . . .

2

Losing Courage before Difficulties

> Courage is not limited to the battlefield or the Indianapolis 500 or bravely catching a thief in your house. The real tests of courage are much quieter. They are the inner tests, like remaining faithful when nobody's looking, like enduring pain when the room is empty, like standing alone when you're misunderstood.
>
> —CHARLES SWINDOLL

Introduction

My brothers and I loved to go and visit our Grandpa and Grandma Keiser. They lived in an old two-story house by the mill pond on the Pine River, so there were plenty of things for us to do in their backyard. And we loved to tear through the house, chasing pirates or rustlers or desperadoes of one kind or another, before settling down at the kitchen table for a Nehi soda. Since we all loved both grape and orange, there was little squabbling about who got what to drink. After all, we tried to be as accommodating as possible for kids ages four, eight, and nine. I was eight.

The only restriction placed on us was that we were not allowed to go upstairs at any time. Grandpa and Grandma had a modest two-story house. All the bedrooms were upstairs, and the stairs were narrow and quite steep. In addition, the house had hot water radiators for heat. I'm sure the adults constantly worried that one of the boys would burn himself on a radiator or fall down the stairs—or be pushed. However, since we were not the easiest lot with which to reason, Grampa simply told us that a bear lived upstairs and it would be better to keep away since the bear was both ferocious and hungry. That's all it took. We would stare up the stairs from time to time and listen intently. We were certain that we heard what was surely bear claws scratching in the hallway one Christmas Eve. For us, the upstairs was simply off limits.

Off limits, that is, until my mom went to the hospital to deliver our youngest brother. Since Dad worked the midnight shift, we were to stay the night with Grandpa and Grandma. We played in the backyard and came in at dusk for a soda. All was fine until it was time to go to bed. Grandma told us that we would be sleeping upstairs. "No way!" we protested, "we do not want to be eaten by the bear!" "Oh, you won't," Grandma tried to console us, "the bear left a few days ago to make room for you. There's no bear in the house now." But we simply could not be convinced. In fact, we were almost sure that we had heard the bear upstairs earlier that very evening. "Fine," Grandpa said, "I'll take care of that * * * bear." He marched out of the room and came back a few minutes later with a loaded shotgun. "Just stay here," he told us, and up the stairs he went, carefully stocking his prey. All of a sudden, *boom!*—we heard a very loud blast from the shotgun. It made our ears ring! Grandpa came back down the stairs with a smoking gun and announced that the coast was clear. The bear had apparently jumped out the window and ran away just as Grandpa took a shot at him. "He won't be back," we were assured, "bears are very afraid of guns, and rightfully so."

After several rounds of negations, it was agreed that we three boys would all sleep in the same room. Slowly, very slowly, we started up the stairs. "Have courage," Grandpa told us, "it's all in your imagination." "I know I am supposed to have courage," I whimpered, "but right now, I'm full of fear!" "Well," Grandpa replied in an unexpected act of kindness, "sometimes it's okay to have both. Just stay together and keep climbing." That we did, and after looking in every room and under every bed, we were convinced that the bear was really gone. "But what if the bear comes back?" we queried. "Won't happen, but if he does, he'll have to answer to me," Grampa said with a single-minded look in his eyes, still holding the shotgun. With that assurance, we locked the door, turned off the lights, jumped into bed, and went to sleep. To the best of our knowledge, the bear never came back. Nevertheless, we kept our distance and played in the backyard as much as possible.

***

In this chapter, we will explore what happens when we face difficulties, why it is easy to lose courage in the process, the unintended consequences for doing so, and what we can do to get back on track. At some time or other, it happens to most of us. And as we shall see, courage does not mean the absence of fear. In fact, sometimes the greatest test of courage is precisely when we are facing the bear, real or imagined. As my grandfather told a frightened trio of young boys that formative evening, "Just stay together and keep climbing." That's good advice for all of us.

Facing Difficulties

Before we explore the ramifications for losing courage before difficulties, let's focus a bit on the difficulties we face and our hidden assumptions and theologies that can drive us to guilt, shame, doubt, and despair. First, it is important to note that there are different kinds of difficulties, and it is important to make a distinction between them. A difficulty can be a *thing* that is hard to accomplish, understand, or deal with; a problem, handicap, impediment, obstacle, stumbling block, or barrier. A difficulty can also be a *situation* that is difficult or even dangerous; a predicament, a hard time, or a real mess like being caught in the middle between two angry or nasty persons. The distinction is important to keep in mind as you face difficulties and attempt to navigate your way through them. For example, if the difficulty is due to a handicap or impediment, the primary strategy may be accommodation. The clarifying and driving question becomes this: how can I deal with this difficulty, knowing full well that I can't make it go away? It is a difficulty that has certain parameters that will not change, regardless of our desire to the contrary.

On the other hand, a difficulty may be a messy situation with your boss or a coworker, and it is easy to assume that the situation cannot change—even though in reality it can. In essence, you say to yourself, "These are the cards that I've been dealt, and there is nothing I can do about it." Of course, the problem is that in doing so you simply become the victim, going through the motions without any hope or intention of making a correction or a difference. For example, how many times have you heard someone say, "I'm just not good at . . ." (You put in the last word.) It could be math, music, public speaking, planning, or hospitality; any number of things. In many cases, your fixed mind-set becomes a self-fulfilling prophesy. For example, studies in mathematics education have demonstrated that children who think they are not good at math consistently do worse in developing math skills than their peers who believe that they can learn math, even though their ability levels are essentially the same. And the same goes for teachers of mathematics, too. Why? Because a closed mind-set (I'm not good at this and I can't change, or you can't change) demotivates, intimidates, and invites fear, viewing each difficulty as just another chance to fail rather than another opportunity to grow and develop. The operative word becomes "I can't" and if you really believe you can't, you probably won't.

Certainly, difficulties come in all shapes and sizes. Much can be said about having the right mind-set. Not all barriers and situations are unchangeable. In fact, many are, so it is important to examine each one and deal with it accordingly. If you perceive and react to each and every difficulty in exactly the same way (what we might call a fixed pattern of response), you will most likely add to your list of difficulties rather than reduce it. In the midst of difficulties, there is much to be said for an open mind-set: new difficulty, new day, new opportunity!

Regardless of your personal approach to difficulties, the truth of the matter is that they will come. Honestly, it is just a part of life, the rent we all pay for living and caring in this world. And they are neither fun nor easy, particularly so when they are not of our own doing. When the actions of others introduce change, uncertainty, or mistrust into our lives, they often lead to difficulties, and that can bring on bouts of self-pity and blame. "Why me? I don't deserve this. It's not my fault!" is the lament. And while all this may be true, it does not change the fact that you are facing a difficulty that adds complexity and anxiety to your day, and that reality can drain away your joy, energy, and focus. At the end of the day, it matters little who is responsible for the difficulties you face. You have to face them nonetheless.

And at times we create our own difficulties, becoming our own worst enemy. Most of us can identify with Mark Twain, who once quipped: "I have lived a long life and had many troubles, most of which never happened." Why is it that we let things go to our imaginations, seeing things as much worse than they really are? You don't hear from someone for a week or two, and you begin to worry that they are mad at you for some unexplained reason. You have to take a driving test, and you just know that you will fail. The boss wants you to drop by her office for a minute, and you worry that you are about to be fired. You have an ache or pain, and your mind goes to the "C" word. We can all look back to times when we have caused stress and worry for ourselves and others unnecessarily, creating real difficulties from events that never happened.

Another complicating factor when facing difficulties is our own embedded theology of circumstances. As we attempt to answer questions about why bad things happen and difficulties arise, our underlying understanding of God is revealed. In Old Testament times, the prevailing understanding was that you had to have a special arrangement with God. If you were good and obeyed his laws, then he would bless you and your work. Your family would grow and be healthy, the rains would come, your crops would flourish, and your herds would multiply. It was a productive partnership. But if someone sinned, then bad things happened. Droughts came, crops failed, businesses collapsed, and conquering armies arrived at the gates. In so many instances, this Old Testament understanding of God leaks into our lives even today, bringing a layer of complications to the difficulties we face. For example, if difficulties are the result of our failure or sin, then surely that sin must be addressed before things can get better. Certainly, Job's friends suggested as much, and it happened to my good friend, Dana, too. He was suffering from a terminal brain tumor with only weeks to live, and a well-meaning person flew from Albuquerque to San Diego just to take him to lunch and inform him that his tumor was obviously the result of some unconfessed sin in his life, so his only recourse was to confess his sins and hope that God would rescind the punishment. What a sick, sick understanding of God, and what a hurtful thing to say to a godly, dying man. Of course, some of our difficulties may be a direct result of our own rebellion and sin, but it is a terrible mistake to label every difficulty as a punishment from an angry God. When we do, we bring in an unnecessary and unhelpful layer of guilt, shame, and condemnation to our lives, and an uninvited distance between God and us.

At other times, we view our difficulties as a message or a test from God. That is, the reason for the difficulty is that God wants to send us a message or test us to see if we are good enough or able enough to enjoy eternal favor. This can also lead to pain and guilt, especially if we are having difficulty dealing with the difficulty. Of course, I believe that God communicates with us in many ways, but to understand a terminal illness of a beloved family member or the fatal car accident or someone's business failure as God's way of trying to get our attention or testing our character both underestimates the love and wisdom of God and overestimates our own place in the tragedy. To be clear, God can and does work through all kinds of difficulties, pain, and suffering to bring grace, healing, and hope, but God is not in the business of bringing tragedy to someone just to get their attention or to send a message. God certainly has more direct and loving methods at his disposal.

I want to discuss one final theological complication when facing difficulties that confounds our ability to address them effectively (although there are many more that could be named), what I call the "perfect plan" understanding of life. In this theology of circumstance, God has a perfect plan for your life, and your job is to find it and walk along that singular path. When you do, all is good. Difficulties come when you stray from the path, so when they do come you spend your time and energy trying to figure out what wrong turn you took rather than trying to address the difficulty that you face. In my view, it adds, at best, an unhelpful layer of complexity to the situation, and at worst, a sense of despair, viewing the difficulty as a sign that you have lost your way.

For others, another aspect of the "perfect plan" idea is the understanding what whatever comes is God's plan. Our job is to be patient and tolerant, to just take it, knowing that we may never know the reason for our difficulties. I sat down at breakfast in the university dining hall one day across from the student. "How's it going today?" I asked. "Not very well," was the response. "I stubbed my toe on the sidewalk this morning and it really hurts." She was wearing sandals, prominently displaying a swollen red and blue big toe. "Wow!" I gasped, "that looks painful." "Yes, it is," she said, "but I'm not worried. I'm sure that this is all a part of God's plan for me." I was honestly stunned. Finally, I summoned up this response: "I do want to be sympathetic to your situation, but I don't think God has a plan for your big toe. You are not being called to a Toe Ministry in Tasmania. If there is any message here, it is for you to pick up your feet and be careful where you walk, or wear different shoes!" Now, to be clear, I am not in any way trying to make light of a mangled toe. I do know that a toe injury can be very painful, but to spiritualize it and accept it as the work of God misses the point completely. While the consequences for doing so in this instance are quite minimal, they can be quite high, even debilitating, in more extreme difficulties. And they can shape your relationship with God and deform your theology for years to come.

Honestly, when facing difficulties, it is arduous enough to summon our courage without complicating the situation with faulty theology. At the end of the day, we have to confess that difficulties are unwanted, and at times they can be terrible—just awful. What is needed in such circumstances is not blame, guilt, recrimination, despair, and self-loathing, but rather a clear head, perspective, and will. To be fair, I do not know why all the things that happen to us happen. None of us do. But I am confident that God is not an angry puppeteer, pulling strings to make us dance at every divine whim. I do know that life is messy for all of us from time to time, and when it is, where is God? Not up in the air pulling strings, but right in the mess with us, bringing grace, healing, and hope. So, life is messy; it either is, has been, or will be. You can count on it. That's life. But I have also learned that God is faithful. You can count on that, too.

So, the challenge is to not turn coward before today's difficulties. When Jesus sent his disciples out, he sent them out as sheep among wolves. To be sure, there were wolves out there, so they were cautioned to be careful. Be as wise as serpents and as innocent as doves, Jesus told them (Matt 10:16). There is much to be learned in the midst of difficulties, and it will build character if you give it half a chance. With the proper mind-set, facing difficulties can be an opportunity to grow and develop, to become aware of unused or unknown talents, and to gain valuable life experiences and perspectives. Lessons can be learned that bring insight, empathy, and humility. It is always helpful to think about what God is trying to teach you (about yourself or about God), for there is much to be learned from any experience. As the motto for Upward Bound tells us: If you can't get out of it, then get into it! That's good advice for all of us when we face difficulties. Truly, mind-set, worry, and poor theology can complicate matters a good deal in the midst of difficulties, so the key is to lean in. However, I have come to believe that the most debilitating thing that causes us to lose courage is fear. That's where we'll turn our attention next.

Fear

I would say that the greatest impediment to facing our own difficulties is fear. Fear works on us in several different ways, and it can rob us of the courage to squarely face the day. Actually, there are different kinds of courage: physical courage, moral courage, even spiritual courage. It has to do with the ability to summon resolve and to maintain clarity in the face of adversity. However, fear works on all three to leave us timid, anxious, nervous, and weak. As Proverbs 24:10 points out, "If you falter in a time of trouble, how small is your strength!" Quite true, but how does fear cause us to lose courage?

First, remember that the basic human response to fear is *fight or flight*. They are automatic responses. That is, when we're afraid, we seek to run away or lash out without much forethought. One response is not necessarily more courageous or wiser than the other. It depends on the circumstances, and the correct course of action is usually only evident in hindsight. That is to say, fear makes us shortsighted when we fight or flee without purpose or direction. And some of us respond to fear by freezing in place or wrapping ourselves in a blanket of denial, or sadly, both, leading us to ignore, minimize, rationalize, and blame. When this happens, fear is no friend.

One fear that does not fit neatly into any category (physical, moral, spiritual) is the fear of failure, precisely because it touches on all three at such a very deep level. Of course, no one is eager to fail, and failure in the form of losing a home or a job or your standing in your church or community is so devastating because it is these things that give us our identity and provide a sense of self-worth in our culture. We are enmeshed in a culture whose primary values are appearance, achievement, and affluence, and when we are faced with losing any of these, fear rages because it threatens so deeply and directly our sense of who we are and how others regard us.

And to complicate matters even more, fear also has several unintended consequences. The first unintended consequence is that without courage, the practice of other virtues tends to give way. That is, when fear dominates, it not only drives our courage and resolve underground, it also makes our practice of other virtues erratic at best. We are less able to be consistently generous, forgiving, honest, or kind—in effect, making our lives less humane. And the results can be devastating. Just when we are in such need of supportive relationships, our actions isolate us and push others away. Courage, I have come to believe, is one of the stabilizing factors in our lives, the glue that holds things together.

A second unintended consequence of fear is that it can lead us to talk one way in public and another way in private, what my dad would call being "two faced." I've witnessed faculty members gather in the hallway after a meeting with the president to express their disgust, anger, and disagreement, even though they smiled and said nothing in the meeting. This is an example of "the meeting after the meeting." Of course, the problem with this is that the president goes away from the meeting thinking that all are in agreement with her new plans and the faculty feel better by venting, but there is no public acknowledgment of a disagreement or any way to move forward effectively. Fear reigns, and the result is organizational dysfunction.

A third consequence of fear is playing both sides against the middle because we are more concerned with gaining approval than speaking the truth. Rather than taking a stand, we pull back and express different opinions and concerns depending upon the group we are with, saying what we think others want to hear. Ultimately, playing both sides against the middle is actually a form of cowardice. It happens when we lose courage in the face of difficulties, and when we do so we lose part of ourselves, too.

The good news is that courage can guide our actions in the midst of our fears. Courage compels us to stay in the fight when the stakes are high—or eternal. As my grandfather taught me many years ago, "It is perfectly natural to be afraid of the bear, but just don't let the bear win. Stay together, climb the stairs, and get a good night's sleep." Courage, it seems, is not the opposite of fear or the absence of fear, but rather a steadfast lean in the face of fear. It is being afraid and climbing the stairs anyway.

Quiet Tests of Courage

So, courage is a steadfast lean in the face of fear. Quite true, but does that mean that courage is only summoned in the face of a great flood or a burning building or an angry bear. No. There are inner tests of courage, too, quiet tests that summon a steadfast courage of another sort. It is not the courage it takes to risk your life while performing some type of heroic act in the face of eminent danger, but rather the courage to maintain your integrity and self-respect in the face of difficulties, attacks on your character, and downright failure. The epigraph at the beginning of this chapter highlights three of them: remaining faithful when nobody's looking, enduring pain when the room is empty, and standing alone when you're misunderstood. In my view, these are much more difficult and transformative than jumping off a bridge to save a drowning victim. No one is looking and there will be no praise or medals for doing so. These are quiet tests of inner courage that challenge you to the core and shape your character; they reveal who you really are. And it is rarely easy, and not always pretty.

Maintaining integrity in the midst of difficulties takes courage, one of our most important and essential life tasks we will face. I have come to believe that while we are not always as successful in these tasks as we would like to be, we can grow and learn from all our experiences and from the supportive friendships of others, too. It is an ongoing process of summoning the courage to say no, to tell the truth, to do the right thing, to return good for evil, to hold your tongue, to get up again, to walk away, or to end the day with the resolve to face the next. It is the quiet courage to set your face like a flint (Isa 50:7), and trust in a God who is there when everyone else is not. It is trust in the God who tells us to not be afraid in the middle of the night (over 350 times in the Bible), to stand firm but not still, to wait, watch, and listen, and to learn. It is trust in the God who told Joshua, "As I was with Moses, so I will be with you; I will never leave you nor forsake you" (Josh 1:5). With all my heart and mind, I believe that God promises the same for us. In our darkest, most lonely hours, God is with us. It is from this knowledge that we summon the resolve to face the quiet tests of courage, to struggle with the difficulties of today and still muster the courage to face tomorrow.

And as we do so, we will find that slowly, steadily, and surely, we are molded in the image of Christ. In the lonely days and quiet nights when we feel that we are as low as we can go, something real and honest is happening, something that may not be recognized or appreciated for days or even years to come. Such experiences, while neither requested nor desired, touch our very core and shape us in very deep ways. If we do not turn coward before such difficulties, we can emerge as different persons—more sensitive to God's leading, more insightful to the events around us, and more sympathetic to the needs of others, particularly those who are walking on roads that we have traveled. Without question, difficulties do challenge us, and they can hurt us, too, but they can also change us—if we face them with courage and resolve.

Scripture

In the previous section, I referenced God's promise to Joshua and suggested that it is a promise for each of us, too, but before we turn to some practical advice in the face of difficulties, I want to briefly look at two very familiar Bible stories: the story of Shadrach, Meshach, and Abednego, and the story of David and Goliath. These two stories can be enlightening to all of us who are struggling to maintain courage in the face of difficulties.

The Fiery Furnace

Most of us will remember the story of the three young men in the fiery furnace—Shadrach, Meshach, and Abednego, placed there by King Nebuchadnezzar because they would not follow his decree to kneel down and worship his gold idol (Dan 3). And we recall that when the king looked into the fiery furnace, he saw not three but four men walking around in the fire unharmed. What a sight! It is an inspiring story of three young men remaining faithful to their beliefs and values in the face of power, coercion, narcissism, and certain death. They did not turn coward before these very real difficulties. However, I want to point out an often-overlooked statement they made just before they entered the fiery furnace. After telling the king that they believed that their God could and would deliver them from this difficulty, they said, "But even if he does not, we want you to know, Your Majesty, that we will not serve your gods or worship the image of gold you have set up" (Dan 3:18). *Even if he does not . . .* What a powerful testimony. We believe that he can and will directly intervene and change our circumstances. We hope, pray, and trust that he will. But even if he doesn't, we still trust and believe! This, it seems to me, is the way to face difficulties without losing courage when things do not go our way. God is not absent. We don't always know why bad things happen or why difficulties come our way, but we can be sure that he is with us and at work in us, bringing grace, healing, and hope to our situation—even when the situation is awful. May we all have an "even if" trust in God.

David and Goliath

When I was growing up, my hero was David—not King David, but David the shepherd boy who killed Goliath with a slingshot. I would reenact the scene in our backyard, using a rug hanging on the cloths line to represent the enemy. Of course, I didn't have King Saul's armor and helmet to wear or his sword to carry, but then David did not use them either. He tried them on, but couldn't even move (1 Sam 17:38–40). In the end, he took his sling and five smooth stones, carried the fight to the giant, and walked into the history books. It is a marvelous story of maintaining courage before difficulties.

It is also instructive to all of us who are facing difficulties of one kind or another. The king wanted David to use his personal armor and sword. In other words, he wanted David to look like him and fight like he would (even though he didn't have the courage to go out there himself), but David didn't let others define him (dress him up as a battle-tested warrior) or his difficulty. Instead, he used the gifts and graces that he had, a sling and mobility, the fighting skills of a shepherd. This is a valuable lesson for all of us. In the midst of difficulties, we can receive a good deal of advice of this kind: "If I were you . . ." or "Let me tell you what you should do . . ." Of course, these advice givers are well-meaning and possibly correct, but in every case, it is important to remember that they are not you. You have unique gifts and graces. Don't let those standing on the outside define the nature of your problem or insist on a solution that is not you.

Some Practical Advice

Before we conclude this chapter with some questions for reflection and discussion, let me offer a few words of practical advice to maintain courage in the face of difficulties. Honestly, what I have to offer is not earth-shaking, but hopefully it will be helpful.

Don't Let Fear Drive Your Actions

It is so easy for us to overplay our fears. Our first inclination will be to either run and hide or lash out. These are, as we have already discussed, quite natural and normal responses, but actions grounded in fear often limit us from seeing other ways of understanding our difficulties or possible ways to deal with them—or if need be, to endure them. When we face difficulties and our fears arise, it is important to take a step back, gather a deep breath, survey the territory, and look for guidance, knowing that we can be fearful and courageous at the same time. We do not have to let our fears rob us of our insights or our sense of the present. We just stay together and keep climbing. The worst thing we can do in the face of fearful difficulties is to hide, even when everything inside us is screaming to do just that.

Check Your Theology

In times of difficulty, it is important to watch our talk—our god-talk. Poor theology, as we have discussed, makes bad situations worse. In difficult times, it is a temptation to let others define who God is or what God is up to in your situation. Don't let anyone put God or your circumstances into their theological box. Keep your focus of the fact that a loving God is with you, and set your face like a flint. He will neither leave you or forsake you, no matter what others say.

Guard against Negative Self-Talk

In times of difficulties, we often are flooded with our own negativity, with demeaning self-talk: "I'm just stupid; I guess I had it coming anyway; Maybe I'm not supposed to be happy; I don't deserve a second chance; I just can't get a break; The cards are stacked against me." When our world is rocked, we are absolutely flooded by thoughts of all kinds. It is easy to be both surprised and overwhelmed (even shamed) by such unsolicited negativity bubbling up in our spirit, swirling inside our mind, and coming out our mouth. Remember, just because such thoughts come, it doesn't mean that they are true, and we certainly don't have to act on such ideas. Just acknowledge them and let them go, and if you can't, talk to a close friend or spiritual advisor. Deal with them squarely so such ideas don't deal with you.

Use Your Own Gifts and Graces

It is important to remember that you have to deal with your difficulties with the gifts and graces you have, not the ones that you or others wish you had. Remember the story of David the shepherd boy. He couldn't fight Goliath in King Saul's armor. In fact, he couldn't even move! But he did have some gifts and graces at his disposal, the tools and skills of a shepherd. So with resolve, a sling, and five smooth stones, he looked the giant in the eyes and took him out. Be clear about your own gifts and graces, and use them in good times and bad times, too. Be who you are—no one else has had more practice.

Maintain Integrity on the "U" Journey

Most of our trials and difficulties will take the form of a U. We go down. We fall. Sometimes it is a gradual decent, but more times than not it is a rapid trip to the bottom, the result of the loss of a job or a loved one, a serious illness, a horrible boss, a moral failure, or some other sort of blow. Whatever the reason, we hit bottom very quickly and the landing is painful. We find ourselves in a daze, wounded, and trying to pick up the pieces of a career, a marriage, a friendship, or a dream. And as much as we want such occasions to be short in duration, they are usually not. We don't just fall and then spring up to the surface again like a bobber. Instead, there is a road ahead that we must walk. Some call it the Emmaus Road—the road of disappointment. It is the bottom of the U. Hopefully, at some point, we will rise again—slowly, steadily, and surely—different and better persons for it.

But while on the road called disappointment, the temptation to rationalize, blame, attack, disrupt, cut corners, criticize, even steal and lie, is huge. It is incredibly easy to justify such actions as compensation for how we have been treated. Maintaining your integrity at the bottom of the U will take the rawest kind of courage, but there is no better way to be formed in the likeness of Christ than to travel with him from Good Friday to Easter Sunday. You see, he, too, had a U journey of eternal consequence.

If Necessary, Hit the Reset Button

It also takes real courage to recognize when it is time to hit the reset button and move on. Most of this chapter has been devoted to times when you find yourself stuck in a ditch or forced to swim upstream. It is in these times when it is important to set your jaw and lean in, resolute to maintain your integrity and make the best of it, knowing that God is with you and working in you. However, there are times when the stream is terribly toxic. No matter how much resolve and courage you have, such streams will only hurt you. They will make you sick. In such instances, the wise thing to do is to hit the reset button and move on. Get out of the stream and find safer waters.

Conclusion

In this chapter, we first looked at difficulties and the havoc that hidden assumptions and misguided theologies can play in times of personal crisis and outright failure, particularly the idea that God is good to us only if and when we are perfect. Next, we examined the role that fear can play in losing courage, and affirmed that we can be fearful and courageous at the same time. In fact, in most instances when real personal courage must be summoned, fear is present, too. We just don't let it prevent us from doing what we know to be right—stay together and keep climbing—one step at a time. We also discussed the quiet tests of courage, tests that in the last analysis expose our character and provide an opportunity for either failure or growth. These are perhaps the toughest times we will ever face.

After a brief look at two stories from the Old Testament, the Fiery Furnace and David and Goliath, we agreed that we must face our difficulties with the gifts and graces we have, not the ones we wish we had. And at the end of the day, it is not our successes that measure our courage but rather the resolve to remain faithful regardless of the outcome.

Finally, we concluded this chapter with some words of practical advice, and suggested that most of us will traverse the U at one time or another. There is a fall or steep descent, a long walk on the road called disappointment, and a steady, slow rise. It is in and through these difficulties that we are shaped and formed in Christ's image. He, too, walked the U—from that horrible Friday to that glorious Easter Sunday morning.

Questions for Reflection and Discussion

1. Why do we tend to isolate ourselves in times of difficulty when we are in such need of support, encouragement, and the wisdom of others? Is it embarrassment, shame, or something else? And why is it so easy to see others in a tough or terrible situation and say or do nothing? What can we do for those who are facing deep difficulties?

2. Can you think of instances when you saw or experienced faulty theology at work during times of difficulties, making things worse?

3. When the negative voices bubble up in your own life, what are they saying about you and to you? What can you do about such voices?

4. Why are the inner tests of courage so difficult for all of us, and yet they are the most formative? What inner test of courage are you facing right now, or have you faced in the past?

5. What would you say are your gifts and graces? Do you feel that they are fully utilized?

6. When someone falls and you know that they have entered the U and are about to walk the road called disappointment, what can you do to be a faithful presence in his or her life? What could others have done for you in such times? Do you have enough courage to ask for help?

FOR TODAY

O God:
Give me strength to live another day;
Let me not turn coward before its difficulties . . .

3

Proving Recreant to Duties

> I long to accomplish a great and noble task, but it is my chief duty to accomplish small tasks as if they were great and noble.
>
> —HELEN KELLER

Introduction

When I graduated from college, I headed to Kansas City to attend seminary, and I took a job as a part-time teller working the drive-thru at a nearby Commerce Bank to make ends meet. As it turned out, I found work at the bank to be much more life-giving than seminary study, and within a year I was a full-time employee; and six months later, I was made an officer of the bank, overseeing the tellers, the vault, the drive-thru, all backroom operations, and even making a loan or two. To be honest, my meteoric rise to the management of the bank was due primarily to the fact that the bank's parent company was in rapid expansion mode that created a severe management shortage. I was just in the right place at the right time, and soon had a desk in the main lobby of the bank and a light blue blazer with the Commerce Bank logo stitched on the vest pocket. The officers of the bank faithfully wore their blazers each Friday, and I did so with a particular sense of satisfaction and not a small amount of pride. Before too long, it all went to my head.

It all came out sideways one sweltering Friday afternoon in early July. It was over 100° and the humidity was oppressive. I was sitting at my desk in the lobby, wearing my blue blazer, when my phone rang and I learned that a customer in the drive-thru tried to send through a canister full of coins. The canister was now stuck in the pneumatic tube, and someone had to go outside with a large, black plastic hose and push the canister through to the teller. It was simply hard, dirty work, and particularly so in such hot and humid conditions. I looked around to see who could go out and do the dog work, but everyone was busy waiting on customers. It was a very busy Friday afternoon, so I would have to go out myself, but I had the distinct feeling that it was a bit beneath my blue blazer dignity and status. I got up and fretted my way to the back of the bank.

As I walked through the check-filing area, I had a great idea. There sat Karl, a quiet man in his mid-sixties, carefully filing checks away as was his job. I walked over to Karl and said, "Karl, the drive-thru is stuck again. Please get the black hose out of the backroom and go out and push it through right away. Customers are waiting." He looked up at me calmly and said, "I'm sorry, but I don't believe that that is my job to do." "You're right," I snapped without thinking, "but I'm telling you to do it, so that makes it right." He smiled sadly and spoke quite slowly, "There have been times when I had to do whatever I was told to do, I had no choice, but now I just want to do what I was hired to do. I'm sorry."

It seemed to me that the work stopped in the room and all ten employees were staring at me. *How dare he question my authority? I am, after all, a blue blazer!* raced through my mind. I flashed a not-so-kind smile and raised my voice so everyone in the room could hear, "I am an officer of this bank, and I have given you a direct order. So, you either pick up the black plastic hose and get out there and push the canister through, or pick up your personal belongings and leave this bank. You either do what I say or you are fired!" Having ended that ugly speech, I spun around and started to walk back to my desk in the lobby.

I didn't get more than six or seven paces, however, until I began to slow down and finally stop. I leaned my forehead against the wall, knowing what I had to do. I had to go back and make things right, so I returned to the check-filing room. The room grew quite once again. "Karl," I began contritely, "I'm sorry. I had no right to speak to you that way, and you are right that pushing the canister through to the tellers is not your job. Please forgive me." "Of course," was his reply without even an upward glance. I went to the storage room, got out the hose, lugged it over to the drive-thru, and started pushing the canister through the pneumatic tube. I was already in a full sweat when I saw Karl walking toward me, starting to take off his suit jacket. "Oh, no, Karl," I said, motioning him to go back inside the air-conditioned building. "This is not your job." "I know," he said with a smile, "but I don't mind helping you out. Think of me as a volunteer." So, together we pushed the canister full of coins to the teller, and business returned to normal.

As Karl and I were cleaning the black grime from our hands with a wet towel in the restroom, I noticed that he had some numbers tattooed on his wrist, and suddenly his remark about having to do as he was told without recourse and his reluctance now to be ordered around made perfect sense to me. "Oh, Karl, does that mean what I think it means?" I asked. "Yes," he said softly, "I was in the camps, but that is all in the past. Now I work for the bank and for you." Again I said, "Please, please forgive me, Karl. I didn't know."

He did.

* * *

I learned some valuable lessons that day. I learned that when you prove recreant in your duties, even small duties, you are diminished, and you diminish others, too. I learned that power can easily go to your head, and when it does, you can lose sight of the task at hand. I learned that even when you come up terribly short, there can be grace and healing at work, often at the most unexpected times and from the most unexpected places. The key is to stop, turn around, go back, and make it right. It isn't often easy, but it is always the right things to do. And I learned a great deal about the Holocaust, too, choosing it as the topic for one of my major papers in my graduate program. Guess who served as the primary source for the paper, and introduced me to a group of survivors whose stories gave real depth and a personal dimension to my work? Yes, it was Karl. He volunteered a second time, and I humbly accepted his help again.

In the last chapter, we examined how losing courage in the face of difficulties can be avoided. In this chapter, we will look at what it means to prove recreant to duties, something very easy to do in difficult times. And we'll think together about how to avoid some of the pitfalls that come our way, and what to do if we're already in the ditch. Together we'll pray, "Oh God: Give me strength to make it through another day. Let me not turn coward before its difficulties or prove recreant to its duties." As we shall see, it is in the little things and small tasks that our character is shaped and formed.

Duties

Thankfully, this is not a chapter about the everyday, garden-variety kind of procrastination. To be honest, we all procrastinate at some time or other for one reason or another, and some of us are actually quite good at it, probably because we've had a lot of practice. In fact, procrastination can become an art form, an expression of our own personal style, but it can become a very bad habit, too. I don't think that procrastination is necessarily a sin, but not much good can be said for it either, and it can be terribly frustrating to those close to you and personally detrimental in far too many circumstances.

In this chapter, however, we will be examining procrastination of a different kind, a more serious kind, what the *Merriam-Webster Dictionary* defines as being "slow or late about doing something that should be done: to delay doing something until a later time because you do not want to do it, because you are lazy, etc." Note that we are speaking here about postponing until later that which should be done, must be done, now. It is a matter of duty, so we're not speaking here about just putting something off until later in the day, staying up all night to write a paper, or waiting to mow the lawn until just before the guests arrive. This is about proving recreant to our duties in the midst of difficulties, even when the consequences for doing so are sobering. It is procrastination on steroids.

Duty can be thought of as a legal, moral, or social obligation; a responsibility that you are to do or a commitment that you are required to keep. It can also be a task that you are required to perform such as a job, assignment, charge, mission, or role. When I served as university provost (academic dean), I had many duties: attending plays, lectures, and concerts, bringing words of greeting at various functions, hiring and evaluating faculty and staff, planning for accreditation visits, providing developmental opportunities for new faculty, showing up at donor and board of trustee functions, speaking at faculty functions, and attending more committee meetings than you could shake a stick at. Obviously, many duties and obligations came with the position as the chief academic officer of the university, and no one had to remind me to do them. They were simply the duties that came with the position. I must admit, however, that during some painful times at work (I shared some of these difficulties in the introduction), it became very challenging to simply do my duty, to show up. Honestly, I just wanted to stay home and fill out some sudoku puzzles. My passion, my focus, my energy, even my sense of commitment to my duties, began to wane, and I started to seriously question my calling. Daily I prayed "For Today," hoping that I would not prove recreant to my duties. It was a difficult and painful time, and on an occasion or two, I did come up short—but I persevered. As we shall see, one or two slipups does not need to sidetrack or derail your entire journey.

Of course, we have important duties beyond the work place, too, perhaps even more important, duties to family, neighbor, and self. I was taught growing up that your word was your bond. Honestly, I'm pretty sure that I didn't understand fully what a bond was, but I knew that it was important to keep my promises, to keep my bond. It was a matter of character, my character. And my parents insisted that telling the truth and keeping your promises would shape you in good ways. I didn't understand that fully either, but I can look back and say that it did. During particularly difficult times, even desperate times, it is so important to tend to our duties, to show up, no matter how we feel about them at the time. And when we do, we are shaped and formed in good ways, godly ways.

As we will see in the next section, we don't often get sideways to our duties in an instant. It is usually a gradual, painful process, something I call the "V." And so is the recovery, the way out. We will look closely at how proving recreant to duties feeds on itself and creates a downward stairway that depletes our spirit and resolve, and strategies to deal with such difficulties when we find ourselves in that lonely and difficult place.

Proving Recreant

In the last chapter, we looked at turning coward before difficulties, and I suggested that this often happens as a result of a sudden crisis or fall. You go down, and you go down quickly. Then, there is a long, painful path to walk, a journey on the Emmaus Road. It is rarely a quick trip, but there is grace and healing in and through the journey. I called it walking the "U." Proving recreant to duties, on the other hand, is not usually such a quick fall, rather a gradual descent or deterioration. It is a downward stairway of small steps that leads us down until we hit rock bottom, and it is a painful process, often requiring a series of small steps to recover. That's why I refer to proving recreant to duties as "walking the V."

Rarely do we walk the "V" because we are lazy or simply do not want to be faithful to our duties. This isn't a case of ordinary procrastination. No, something much deeper is at work here. Despite our earnest desires to the contrary, we just can't seem to find the energy or motivation to attend to our charge, and in a series of small steps we lose our way. We find ourselves empty, stuck, and engaging in a succession of negative behaviors that make matters worse. We walk down the "V," and before we realize it, we are in deep trouble.

When we first face difficulties, an inner voice goes off, urging us to admit defeat, surrender, or just quit and walk away. Such negative self-talk is quite common, and to some extent normal, but it doesn't have to be destructive. That is to say, we can't always stop the voices from going off in our heads, but we don't have to listen to them. The trouble comes when we believe them as if they truly represent reality. In most cases, they do not. Believing these voices can lead to stagnation, boredom, a loss of any sense of direction, and indecisiveness, all of which leave us empty of motivation, and in some cases, without any concern for our duties. We simply do not care, and we probably don't even know why, but we feel strangely empty. Sadly, in many real aspects, we are.

What bubbles up to fill the void is a sad, irritating sense of resentment. We can't quite put a finger on it or explain what it is, but we feel it deeply. I have come to believe that duty without love and passion becomes impersonal, then restrictive, next joyless, and finally visionless. And all of this leads to a sense that our duties do not really matter to anyone, and neither do we. One cannot stay in this state for very long without engaging in a wicked cocktail of negative behaviors that leads to a disintegration of the soul. Along with losing a sense of motivation to attend to our duties, we stop doing the things that keep us whole—integrative activities that keep body, mind, and spirit joined together.

The first thing to go is usually self-care. We stop eating correctly, sleeping consistently, or exercising faithfully. Although we know that these activities are life-giving and necessary for our personal care, we don't pursue them with any sense of vigor. And when we stop caring for our physical body, our spirit suffers, too.

Next, we engage in a set of antisocial behaviors that keep us separated from others, even though deep down we know that we are in need of support, companionship, and friendship. Perhaps it is the superhero image in all of us, a rugged individualism, that urges us to remain solitary and solve our own problems. I don't really know. But I do know that in times of difficulty, it is easy to go into a state of hibernation. We literally stay in bed or cooped up on the couch with the blinds pulled, hoping that the world and all our difficulties will simply go away. They rarely do.

And we tend to isolate ourselves, rejecting invitations and initiatives from those who reach out. We simply want to be left alone, even though we know that it is unhealthy to do so. And we insulate ourselves, too, putting up barriers so that we know little about what is going on. We turn off our phones, ignore social media, and refuse to answer the door. And sometimes we push others away by means of gruff or hurtful or angry talk, even family members who love us the most. Each activity leaves us more alone and separated from the very people who want to extend comfort. Instead of asking for help and support, we actively work to avoid it, and often don't really know why or anticipate the consequences of our actions.

And to add insult to injury, we forgo attention to our spiritual needs, too. We stop praying, reading Scripture, going to church, meditating, listening, serving, and other spiritual practices. Again, even though we know that such activities are nourishing to our souls, we simply can't muster the energy or intent to do that which we know to do. Even though we are thirsty and in need of living water, we behave as if we were camels. I've done it myself. Such is the journey down the "V."

Finally, we hit the bottom of the "V" and we are in deep trouble. The empty void we feel is real, but since nature abhors a vacuum, our life space is now filled with self-pity, blame, bitterness, and resentment. Living in such a space is the fastest way I know to a blowup or burnout. We stop doing the things that hold our lives together, and find ourselves doing things we would never imagine possible: lying, belittling, criticizing, bullying, stealing, cheating, and entertaining addictions of one kind or another, too. These are all terribly self-destructive. At the bottom of the "V" we feel helpless and hopeless. Sadly, we learn that simply killing time not only leads to a neglect of our duties, it kills our spirit, too.

Now, I know that this portion of the chapter will not lead anyone to do the happy dance. It isn't supposed to. I have seen far too many friends and colleagues travel down the "V" and hit bottom. I have also walked with many who have made the slow and difficult climb out, so I know that there is a light at the end of the tunnel. We can get home before dark.

Still, it is important for all of us to face these difficulties squarely. Turning recreant to life's duties has real consequences, and it can happen to someone we love—or to us. With that in mind, we will look to Scripture for guidance and make some practical suggestions on how to avoid walking the "V" altogether, and what to do if we are already well down the slope. Before we do, however, I want us to examine how maintaining a sense of vocation can help us through difficult times, even times when our sense of duty is wavering.

Vocation

Many of us think that a calling from God as something that belongs to the clergy, to those who are called to full-time Christian ministry. They do have a divine calling, to be sure, but I believe that we, all of us, have a calling from God. We all have a sacred calling.

For some of us, our calling is closely tied to our work, our profession, or area of service. Since college, I have sensed a calling to service in Christian higher education. While the exact way this calling has worked itself out over time (from work in student development, to grant writing, to teaching, to administration, and now back to teaching), the call has remained the same. It has provided my life with a sense of true north—not always knowing what I would do next, but always knowing which way I should be heading and why it was important to do so.

For others, the sacred calling in much less specific, having more to do with the kind of persons we are called to be than the specific kind of work we feel called to do. I think of Micah 6:8, "And what does the Lord require of you? To act justly and to love mercy and to walk humbly with your God," and Matthew 22:37–39, "Love the Lord your God with all your heart and with all your soul and with all your mind . . . and love your neighbor as yourself." Actually, these callings apply to all of us. As Christians, we are called to be a certain kind of people, holy people, regardless of the work we do to put food on the table and pay the rent.

Personally, I like to think about our vocation in terms of a summons for a certain time and to a certain place, a divine appointment from God. Regardless of the exact job we have, or if we have a paying job at all, we are all summoned. We are expected to show up with our gifts and graces, and find opportunities to put them to good use—or the opportunities find us, and when they do, we have a deep sense that we are in our spiritual sweet spot.

In times of personal failure, loss, injury, and pain, however, it is so easy to lose our way. We don't think that God is even talking to us, let alone providing any sense of direction for our lives. "Does he even care?" we ask. In such times, in the middle of some very dark, lonely, even horrible places, God's summons to us may be the only beacon of light we have; a glimmer of hope to guide us in the middle of a storm, telling us that we are not abandoned and a safe harbor is near.

Even in less difficult times, ordinary times, having a clear sense of God's summons can bring a certain grounding in the midst of a culture where the driving values are appearance, achievement, and affluence. When it is all about getting to the top, wherever the top is, and to do so as fast as possible, it is easy to lose our spiritual compass. And even if we get to the very top, we find it to be like Disneyland, entertaining in the short run but without any real depth or meaning. It is form without substance, and the shelf life is very short. We look back at our journey and wonder why we ever thought it was worth so much of our time and energy. We have become a success, but in some sad way we have lost our way, and we know that we have not answered God's summons.

A clear and firm sense of vocation can free us from a destructive, competitive view of life and work where only the winners count, and everyone else is a loser. In God's economy, winning and losing are turned on their heads. "So the last will be first, and the first will be last," Matthew tells us (20:16). And our sense of vocation allows us to view time differently, and avoid the temptation to try to be all things to all people. And perhaps most importantly, understanding our work as a summons to a certain place for a certain time unburdens us from the need to be perfect, always successful, always up front, always on the fast track. When we know, deeply know, that we are summoned by God to be a certain kind of person rather than to be a success in a culture driven by appearance, achievement, and affluence, failures and difficulties take on an entirely different meaning. Perhaps Dallas Willard put it best: "You must arrange your days so that you are experiencing deep contentment, joy, and confidence in your everyday life with God."[1] That is the success to which we are called, and when we make this our focus, much of the things that seem so important now will realign or simply go away altogether.

Before I offer some words of practical advice, let's take a brief look at two stories from Scripture that provide some insights into the fruits from

---

1. As quoted in John Ortberg, *Soul Keeping: Caring for the Most Important Part of You* (Grand Rapids: Zondervan, 2014), 88.

remaining faithful, and some of the circumstances that encourage us to prove recreant to our duties.

Scripture

The story of Jonah, a prophet who was swallowed by a great fish, is probably familiar to most of us. It is one of the first stories we learn as children, especially the part about the whale. The second figure, Benaiah, may not be so familiar. As we will see, they both provide deep truths for those of us facing difficult times.

Jonah

Jonah was a prophet living in the northern kingdom of Israel. That was his calling, but when God summoned Jonah to go to Nineveh, the capital city of Assyria, a longtime enemy, to warn them of their impending destruction, he didn't want to go. In some respects, who can blame him? Who in their right mind would want to go to their sworn enemy with entirely bad news? It would be neither popular nor safe, but the summons was clear. God wanted him to go and deliver a message, but Jonah headed in the other direction.

Jonah boarded a ship sailing for the port of Tarshish, but it ran into a terrible storm that ultimately resulted in Jonah being thrown overboard along with most of the cargo. He was subsequently swallowed by a huge fish. There he remained, according to the story, for three nights, giving him plenty of time to reconsider his actions. He did. When he made it back to the shore, his instructions came a second time, and he traveled straight to Nineveh to warn the city that it was to be overrun in forty days.

Much to Jonah's surprise, however, all the inhabitants of the city, including the king, repented, so God showed mercy and called off the catastrophe. This made Jonah really mad. Suffering from a combination of exhaustion, pride, embarrassment, and a sense of his own prophetic importance, he wanted God to follow through on the prophecy. He totally failed to see the goodness of God's compassion and grace at work, and even God could not convince him otherwise. The story ends with Jonah wishing he were dead, and he told God as much. Although Jonah delivered the divine message to Nineveh, he ended up disillusioned by

God's goodness and blinded to God's concern for each of us. It is really a sad story in many ways.

I know that many want to argue whether or not this story really happened. Honestly, I don't know and I don't think it matters—there are certain truths to be drawn from the story of Jonah regardless of the accuracy of the historical account. First, when facing challenging duties, it is easy to resist God's call and head off in the wrong direction. I am mindful of difficult times in my own life when although it was clear what God was calling me to do, I ran off in the opposite direction, guided by my own faulty compass. And, as in the case of Jonah, it did not turn out very well. Second, my rebellion not only got me into difficulty, but it hurt those close to me, too. Rebellion from God's summons is rarely a solo act, and each decision we make has its own moral trajectory. Finally, in tough times, it is often difficult to see and appreciate God's grace at work, even when it hits us squarely between the eyes. May we be mindful of the divine summons we receive, accept it willingly, and pursue it faithfully.

So, what happened to Jonah? The story doesn't say. As the story ends, he is sitting outside the city gates, pouting, and proving recreant to his duties. After all, he was a prophet. Didn't he have work to do? I guess he could have just sat there until he died, but I don't think that's what happened. Or he could have gone into the city to celebrate with the Assyrians, but I don't think he was much of a mind to do that either. My guess is that after a while, he got up and started for home. And when he got there, I suppose he took up whatever work he did when he was not out prophesying, and tried to live as a faithful presence in the Micah 6:8 fashion, loving both his God and neighbor with everything he had.

Benaiah

"Benaiah son of Jehoiada, a valiant fighter from Kabzeel, performed great exploits. He struck down Moab's two mightiest warriors. He also went down into a pit on a snowy day and killed a lion" (1 Chr 11:22). This is one of my favorite verses in all of Scripture, and I have thought about it many times. Benaiah came from a family known for bravery and performing the duties they faced. His grandfather had a reputation for being a valiant fighter, and his father was a priest. Benaiah drew strength from them both, and emerged as a trusted leader for King David, becoming captain of his bodyguard. Along the way, he went up against an Egyptian fighter who was over seven feet tall with only a small club, and snatched away the giant's own spear and used it to take him out on the spot. A valiant fighter, indeed!

To be honest, I am not much for fighting lions. That sounds like dangerous business, especially when armed with only a small spear. But if I were to fight one, I would not want to face the lion in a pit, and certainty not on a snowy day. Facing a dangerous beast with limited avenues for escape and on slippery footing is no prescription for success. So, why did Benaiah face the beast in such conditions? Why would he go down in a pit on a snowy day to face the lion? The more I have thought about it, the simpler my own explanation gets. Why did he go down in the pit? Because that's where the lion was, and it was his duty to fight lions. To me, it is really that simple.

When duty calls, we rarely get to design the circumstances to our own liking. That's not the way it works. Sitting around hoping and waiting for better conditions is one of the surest ways to prove recreant to our duties. Our job is to face the lion—wherever the lion is found. That's the legacy of Benaiah. Near the end of King David's reign, he needed someone he could trust to escort his son, Solomon, to the place where he would be anointed as the next king; someone who would fight to protect Solomon or die trying. Who do you think he called upon for such an important task? Ideally, it would be someone who had a record of proving faithful to their duties, whether it was a lion or a seven-foot Egyptian fighter. You're right, he called Benaiah, and Benaiah was there on a moment's notice.

Trust, it seems to me, is built one lion at a time. Our faithfulness in the little things has a cumulative effect on the way others see us, and it shapes our own character, too. As we pray that we will not prove recreant to our duties, we have to face whatever comes our way, even if it happens to be a lion in a pit on a snowy day. Perhaps the most striking example of this I know is the resolve of Jesus as he made his way to Jerusalem. Of course, if circumstances could have been different, that would have been fine with him. He even prayed that it might be so. But in the end, he was determined to answer his summons, even though he knew it would cost him his life. May we be faithful, too, as we face our difficulties, one lion at a time.

Some Practical Advice

Certainly, we do not want to prove recreant to our duties, and there are some simply ways to "get off the dime," as my father was fond of saying. Here are five words of practical advice when we find ourselves stalled in the face of difficulties.

Do Something

When we find ourselves pouting outside the city gates like Jonah or just curled up on the couch with the blinds drawn and the television on, the best thing we can do is to get up and do something—anything. It almost sounds silly, I know, but the first step can be ever so difficult. Even if the first step is to simply mow the lawn or do the dishes or call a friend or write the first paragraph, the key is to do something, and more often than not, one step will lead to another, and another, and another. However, if we wait for inspiration or a change in circumstances, we find ourselves in a waiting game that is totally counterproductive. Do something right now!

One Lion at a Time

It is easy to be overwhelmed when facing a daunting task. When I think about writing, I can get a stomach ache. Along with the little voice in my head that tells me that I have nothing to offer and I am a terrible writer, I hear this, "How in the world will you ever be able to write 250 pages?" Good question. The answer is that I can't write 250 pages, but I can write a paragraph or two for starters. And over time, they will add up. The entire wall is built brick by brick, so start with the first brick.

And it can be awfully depressing when we are pressed by a number of tasks or problems at the same time. There is no way to address them all, at least not at the same time. So, only fight one lion at a time. Isolate the most pressing and important item, and address that one. Then, the next. The rest will have to wait. Running back and forth trying to keep all the plates spinning may be an entertaining sideshow to watch, but it is no way to live. Fight one lion at a time. And I've found that the earlier in the day I fight the lion, the more strength and resolve I have for the battle and the more time I have for recovery. Fight the lion in daylight.

Develop Your Own Early Warning System

Earlier in this chapter, I noted that the loss of motivation and the lack of commitment to important duties rarely happen all at once. Rather, it is usually a gradual step-by-step decline. That is to say, it is more of a "V" than a "U." If this is so, then it is very important to pay close attention to early warning signs of recreant behavior. You have to really know yourself and pay attention to your own delay tactics before these behaviors become seriously debilitating. And it is here where a good friend is so helpful. More often than not, they can see you acting in counterproductive ways long before you realize it yourself. Give them permission to hold you accountable, and listen to them when they do. It sounds simple, but it is hard to do.

Stay in Orbit

Think about a satellite in orbit around a planet. If the satellite gets too close to the planet, gravitational forces will suck it in, causing the satellite to crash and burn. However, if the orbit is too far from the planet, contact is lost and the satellite drifts off into outer space. Getting too close or being too far away both have real consequences. There is a parallel here for those of us who face real difficulties, particularly organizational and relational ones. The key is to stay at a healthy distance, one that allows us to be present without either getting pulled into the mess below or drifting away out of sight and mind. Keep your distance, but remain relevant.

Fill Your Cup Daily

Finally, in the midst of difficulties where we begin to lose our motivation and resolve to continue, it is critical to maintain a routine of self-care. Difficulties produce stress, and stress must be managed or it will eat you alive. Think about what gives you energy, what feeds your soul, and when you feel closest to God. Then, make it an intentional practice to do those things on a daily basis. In the midst of a personal crisis, self-care is often the first thing to go. And when you run out of gas, apathy and indifference soon follow. Fill your cup daily and serve out of the overflow of your life.

Conclusion

In this chapter, we are praying to remain faithful and not prove recreant to our duties. Of course, there are times when we all lose motivation or a sense of urgency about the tasks that await us, and particularly so in difficult and stressful circumstances, but we don't have to succumb to the temptation to simply quit or walk away. There are strategies we can employ, and friends and loved ones we can depend upon to walk with us, hold us accountable, and provide a web of relationships to support us. And even in our darkest times, God's summons can guide us, providing meaning in the midst of the most senseless days. With God's help, we lean into each difficulty, fight the lion, and head for home.

Questions for Reflection and Discussion

1. How would you describe God's calling or summons for your life? Is it general or specific? Can you think of a time it has helped you "stay the course" in the midst of difficult times?
2. What are the early warning signs when your resolve begins to wane? Can you recognize them on your own, or do you need help to do so?
3. Who would be someone you could count on to hold you accountable to your duties? Would you listen to them?
4. When you find yourself "out of orbit," do you tend to fly too close and get caught up in the drama, or simply disconnect and drift away? What strategies could you employ to maintain a healthy orbit?
5. In difficult times, what are the things that fill your spiritual cup, that make you feel God's presence? How could you be more intentional about these spiritual practices on a daily basis? How full is your cup right now? When was the last time there was an overflow?

FOR TODAY

O God:
Give me strength to live another day;
Let me not turn coward before its difficulties or prove recreant to its duties . . .

4

Losing Faith in Other People

> Everyone suffers at least one bad betrayal in their lifetime. It's what unites us. The trick is not to let it destroy your trust in others when that happens.
>
> —SHERRILYN KENYON

Introduction

According to the writer of the great faith chapter in the New Testament book of Hebrews, "faith is confidence in what we hope for and assurance about what we do not see" (11:1). This definition I like very much. Faith is confidence in what we hope for, not confidence in what we already know or have; it is assurance about what we do not see, not assurance in what we have already seen with our own eyes or hold in the palm of our hand. Faith is not about knowledge or sight or possession, but about moving forward nonetheless despite the lack of it. Faith implies some degree of doubt or it would not be faith in the first place. In many ways, they are two sides of the same coin, an inseparable reality of life. Yet we often let our doubts undermine our faith, carrying them secretly as if we had the plague. In this chapter, we'll give faith a careful examination, including the paths that often lead us to lose faith in others and how to maintain a sense of faithful integrity in our lives—but first this story.

* * *

If you want to know a small community and to have the community know you, drive a big yellow school bus. My mother did for years, and when she was in her bus, she was the queen in her castle. She absolutely loved every minute of every trip, whether it was a kindergarten route at noon, the regular morning and afternoon grind, or a special trip with a sports team, band, or choir. I think she particularly enjoyed driving a sports team to an away game when one of her four sons played on the team, but the more I think about it, she adopted so many athletes that she always had sons and daughters aboard. She simply loved her kids—all of them.

She would drive into heavy Detroit traffic and on back country Michigan roads that in wintertime proved to be downright dangerous. She could back that big yellow machine the size of a grey whale into the tightest of places, and she could turn on a dime, avoiding mail boxes, wild life, and even a stray cow or two. I never saw her flinch or even hold her breath. How she ever learned to do so I just don't know. I have trouble backing up and parking my little compact pickup, but she was a natural.

She started driving school buses when my older brother entered high school and started playing sports. Our family always lived on a very tight budget, and my mother knew that we would need some spending money during high school. Of course, my brothers and I talked about getting a part-time job at the local filling station to help make ends meet, but my mother was adamant that she would provide the spending money; we were to play sports. I learned years later that my father was a gifted high school athlete, but his parents thought playing sports was frivolous, so they insisted that he work rather than play sports. In spite of persistent pleas from the varsity basketball coach, he was not allowed to even try out for the team. Instead, he worked as a part-time janitor at the high school, and one of his jobs was to sweep the basketball floor at the half-time of home games. I can't even begin to comprehend the disappointment and humiliation he must have felt. My mother was determined that all four Allen boys would play on the varsity, so she drove a school bus to pave the way.

Many years later, my mother and I had a chance to talk some about her bus-driving days. I wanted to be sure to thank her for driving a school bus all those years so my brothers and I could play sports, and I did. She smiled, acknowledged my gratitude, and started reminiscing about all the trips she took, telling me stories about driving in blizzards on icy country roads with a big ditch on both sides, ditches deeper than the bus itself, and trying to find a suitable parking place for the bus near the old Detroit Tigers baseball stadium. I had heard most of these stories more than once.

In the middle of her monologue, however, she paused and said, "You know, I did drive a school bus so you boys could play sports, but that isn't how I got started. Actually, a year or so before you went to high school, a new educational program was started to help disadvantaged children go to school in the summertime, and, along with instruction, to receive a free hot lunch. We had a large population of migrant workers in our county who picked cucumbers in the summer for the local pickle plant, and they lived in shanty-like huts on the edges of the fields way out in the country. The summer education program was open to their children, but the kids couldn't attend because none of the bus drivers would go out and pick them up. There was real animosity in town toward giving these outsiders summer help, something that many in our small town thought extravagant, misdirected, and downright wrong."

Pausing as if to visualize the events that happened next, she smiled and continued, "So, I said that I would drive out and pick up the kids, and when they pointed out that I didn't have the proper license to drive a school bus, I went over to the next town and got one! Boy, that really made a lot of my friends and neighbors mad. I became invisible. They wouldn't even speak to me. I guess I was sort of being shunned."

"Oh," I added as I leaned in, "you *were* being shunned alright! How in the world did you live with such bigotry? Why didn't you just make them invisible, too?" "Well," she said, "they were my neighbors. You don't give up on them because they're not perfect. None of us are. I guess you just love them—bring a meal when they are sick, sit with them when they mourn, and celebrate with them when they celebrate. And you do the same with their children, and their children—and over time, you know, things have a way of working themselves out."

And work themselves out they did. When my mother died, the little church overflowed with people from all walks of life who wanted to pay their respects: nurses from the hospital, CEOs, corporate attorneys, teachers, shopkeepers, carpenters, farm workers, and neighborhood children. At one time or another, they were all riders on her big yellow bus. And there was a contingent of bus drivers, too, both past and present. When I went to the pulpit to express a few words on behalf of the family, her words reverberated in my soul as I looked out at all the different faces: "You don't give up on them because they're not perfect. . . . I guess you just love them. . . . And over time, you know, things have a way of working themselves out."

* * *

Indeed, they do. It's called grace, and grace never gives up on any of us. There is a lesson here, I believe, for all of us, and particularly for those of us prone to lose faith in other people in the midst of difficult times.

Faith

Before we examine the process of losing faith and ways to maintain what I call a "faithful integrity or wholeness," let's take just a moment to be sure we are on the same page about what we mean when we use the word faith. As you will see, the definition can be complex and at times downright confusing.

Definitions and Uses

When the Apostle Paul wrote to his young assistant, Timothy, he acknowledged that the end was near for himself, and affirmed that "I have fought the good fight. I have finished the race. I have kept the faith" (2 Tim 4:7). And in so many words, he urged Timothy to do the same. What exactly did Paul mean by "the faith"? Would it surprise you to learn that over the centuries there have been some disagreements about the meaning of these words? For many, the faith refers to a proper set of beliefs and convictions, something we call orthodoxy—a belief or way of thinking that is accepted as true or correct. And for some, of course, there is only one correct way, *The Faith*, and you are either right or wrong, in or out, depending on what you believe. Such thinking has led to inquisitions of one form or another for many centuries. Was Paul referring to this type of faith (right belief)? Perhaps. He did urge Timothy to steer clear of false teachings and those who do not tell the truth. Over the centuries, faith and truth have always been interesting traveling companions.

But Paul complicates this idea of faith a bit by asking Timothy to keep his teaching "as a pattern of sound teaching [orthodoxy], with *faith and love in Christ Jesus*" (2 Tim 1:13). So, the faith was not simply a proper set of beliefs for Paul, but also faith in something, or better put, in someone—Christ Jesus. And that faith determines how we conduct our lives (orthopraxy). For Paul, both were extremely important. He was obviously concerned and cautionary about false teachings of various kinds, and he was convinced that the very center of our faith was in Jesus; and that faith, in large part, would determine how we, all of us, make our way in this world.

When Paul wrote that he had kept the faith, I think he probably meant some sense of both orthodoxy and orthopraxy, although he certainly would not have used those words. But there is another aspect of faith that Paul claimed, and I believe that it has much to say to us as we think about losing faith in other people. Faith is also something we have and hold: confidence, complete trust, assurance, hope, and evidence of what is not seen. In this regard, Paul had faith in Timothy. When we pray that we will not lose faith in other people, we are praying for confidence, trust, assurance, and hope in those around us, and it is precisely these things that we can lose or see them slip away during difficult times.

Losing Faith

I've come to believe that all of life is connected in deep and remarkable ways. So, too, is our faith in others; it is connected to our theology and to the way we see ourselves.

Faith in God

Many of us, whether we know it or not, were brought up in religious traditions that explicitly or inexplicitly focused on orthodoxy. In other words, the central aspect in being a Christian was to believe and express the right things, to believe rightly, and to do otherwise was to put your soul in eternal danger and to lose communion with the faithful. Far too often, however, this orthodoxy found its focus on a particular way of viewing the world, reading the Scriptures, understanding the process of salvation and sanctification, or on specific views of creation, the end times, or human sexuality. The list could go on for pages. Others come from traditions that focused more on orthopraxy: taking the sacraments or being baptized in a certain way, keeping the Sabbath or living holy lives—accompanied by a long list of rules, or attending to those on the margins of society. This list could go on for pages, as well. Of course, these are not necessarily bad things, but at times they can serve to isolate and exclude those who practice differently. The point is that it is easy for traditions to major on minors, in effect losing their way, not seeing the forest for the trees.

Sadly, this misdirected focus is not lost on the young. Far too many look back and view these misplaced emphases as patently silly, simply not relevant in our complex world. Time has a way of sweeping away thin theology and beliefs that address neither the realities of life nor the depth of our pain and suffering. A cutout, stand-up God will simply not do; such a foundation cannot hold when the rains come. The result is a slide into disorientation and doubt, and for many, a walk away from their faith altogether. When this happens, the glue is gone that holds together our experiences and the mysteries of life, and the consequence is a lack of assurance or hope or trust in any ultimate sense in anything. And without this sense of something meaningful beyond our own lives, we are left with the lonely task of trying to invent some purpose for who we are, what we do, and why we do it. In our culture, the primary focus is on appearance, achievement, and affluence, and in the pursuit of these transient values, we can easily lose faith in others, believing in them only to the extent that they can help us reach our personal materialistic goals. Loving things and using people can quickly become the order of the day, and when it does, relationships are easily discarded like a pair of old socks.

Faith in Ourselves

As we have just seen, a poor theology or an unnecessary focus on some particularity or peculiarity of belief can have real consequences regarding our faith in other people. And as we shall see, it has real consequences for our faith in ourselves, too. Many hold what I call an "Old Testament View of God" as a great puppeteer. God is seen as vigilant, demanding, petty, needy, judgmental, vindictive, and downright cruel at times, expecting all of us to be perfect and punishing us when we are not. We are left on our own to be good and avoid punishment as best we can. However, deep down we know that we are all flawed, certainly not perfect. So, how can we possibly be good enough to merit God's favor and avoid God's wrath? For many of us, the honest answer is that we cannot. This is more than discouraging, which it is; it can be downright devastating. In keeping with this view, if we are facing difficult times, either we did something wrong (guilt) or something is wrong with us (shame). Certainly, this is a wicked cocktail of blame turned inward, and it wreaks havoc with our well-being and our faith in ourselves.

We tend to project this sense of guilt and shame on others, too. Clearly, they are broken pots as much as we are. In fact, it is easier to see their faults than to see our own. And if we can't trust ourselves, how in the world will we be able to trust others? The answer for many of us is that we can't. Rather than embracing our need for friendship, support, and grace from those close to us in difficult times, we brand them as untrustworthy and shut them out. In doing so, we push away those who are best able to help us in our time of need. And when we do, everyone is diminished. This is more than just having a poor self-concept; we have a poor others-concept, too. The result is a loss of connection and coherence in our lives, and the world is fractured and untrustworthy.

Clearly, our faith in God shapes our faith in ourselves, and both are directly linked to what we believe about others. In the prayer "For Today," we pray that we will not lose faith in other people. It starts by tending the flames of faith in our own lives, keeping hope alive. In the next section, we will look at some practices that can help us maintain and sustain a sense of faithful integrity and wholeness during difficult times; times when losing faith in others becomes a real possibility and comes with real consequences.

Maintaining Faithful Connections

I have tried to make the case that our faith in God, our faith in ourselves, and our faith in others are connected in deep and important ways, so let's look at three practices that can strengthen our faith, and see how they might help us sustain our faith in others during difficult times.

Keeping Vigil

We don't use the word vigil much anymore. It can mean a time of quiet observance, prayer, waiting, or mourning; the act of staying awake at times when sleep is customary. Candlelight vigils are sometimes held to remember the victims of a tragedy or to protest some political or civil action, and certain churches hold vigils on the eve of religious festivals and holy days. Family members keep vigil when a loved one is lost or close to death, and in one way or another we all keep a vigil of sorts when we are waiting for the phone to ring, for someone to make it home in the midst of a nasty storm, or for the doctor to interpret the test results from a biopsy. We wait quietly, often in prayer, sometimes in agony, at times when we would normally be sleeping.

I would like to suggest another understanding for keeping vigil, one that supports and sustains our intent and daily prayer to keep our faith in others during difficult times. What if we committed ourselves to keeping vigil for others? Instead of waiting for the first time they let us down (and, of course, they will because they are a lot like us), what if we committed our time and energy to waiting for their very best to develop, even if it took more than a few sleepless nights, even years? I believe we have a choice in what we wait for; waiting can be an expression of our faith. In fact, sometimes waiting *is* faith. And what if we watched for any indication of the good in others rather than rejecting them at the first sign of failure? What if we made watching for the good in others a daily spiritual practice? As it turns out, we can choose what we watch for, too. And what if we listened for that quiet voice of support and love rather than to the hollow words and empty promises that we all make from time to time? What if we chose to listen for the best in others rather than for overblown, self-serving narratives?

Keeping vigil—waiting, watching, and listening for the good we hope to see in others—is an act of faith, a demonstration of our confidence in what we do not see? I believe that it could change us in profound ways, and it is a choice that we can make. Of course, there will be sleepless, lonely nights, some in agony, some in disappointment, but it is a choice we make to demonstrate our faith in a God who keeps vigil for us and with us, waiting, watching, and listening for any sign of our interest in deepening our relationship with the Eternal.

Remembering Pilgrimage

In one way or another, I think we're all on some kind of pilgrimage. For some, it is a preplanned trip, like a finely crafted tour that goes off like clockwork. Everything falls in place, and we are quick, if we are reflective at all, to thank God for our good fortune and acknowledge just how blessed we are. I have a friend who received an unsolicited job offer while still in school, married the person of his dreams, bought a house, raised a loving family, invested wisely, and retired comfortably—all the while retaining good health and staying active in the local community, school, and church. It is an elegant picture of the American dream with a Christian overlay. I make no particular judgment about this type of pilgrimage, except to say that it is certainly privileged and clearly not the journey that most of us have before us. Life is messy. In all honesty, that is most likely a good thing. Going through life as a tourist is not the most formative way to travel.

The vast majority of us join Abraham, who "when called to go to a place he would later receive as his inheritance, obeyed and went, even though he did not know where he was going. By faith he made his home in the promised land like a stranger in a foreign country" (Heb 11:8–9). Now that's a journey that I can identify with. Most of life does not run like a high-dollar tour of Europe, complete with the best accommodations, a private limo, and a personal tour guide who handles all the details. No, we try to follow God's leading as best we can, but most of the time we have to admit that we do not know where we are going—or why. We simply follow the clues in what seems to resemble a cosmic scavenger hunt, and even when we are clear about God's leading, more times than not we end up living like a stranger in our own land. Pilgrimage, as it turns out, calls us to faith, believing in what we do not yet see and trusting in what we do not yet understand. Pilgrimage is a simple act of faith.

When we understand that we are on pilgrimage, it is natural to travel with a sense of longing; longing for the home we left and for the new life that is still to come. We are travelers between home and home, wandering and wondering what God has in store for us. We often second-guess our decisions. Should we have accepted that job offer, should we have moved to that community, or engaged in that church? When on pilgrimage, striving for clarity and striving with God are quite natural, human responses to the uncertainty we experience on our journey. It is the way we work to manage and understand our lives.

Interestingly, we are often much more forgiving and patient with our own struggles than we are with others when they long, wander, wonder, strive, or question. Particularly in difficult times, it is easy to become impatient and dismiss others as weak in faith, immature, or just plain irritating, especially when they act precisely as we do. When we pray daily that we will not lose faith in others, we must remember that we are all on a pilgrimage of one kind or another. Certainly, we want others to be mindful of our longings and strivings, our journey to find home. But we must be mindful that others are on a pilgrimage, too, and our faith is demonstrated by our commitment to walk with them, even when they don't know where they are going. We walk with and by faith.

Maintaining Hope

In addition to keeping vigil and remembering pilgrimage, there is one more spiritual practice that I believe will be helpful to us as we pray that we will not lose faith in others during difficult times. That is to maintain hope in others, despite the inconsistencies and disappointments they bring our way. But how? I have come to believe that it begins with a resolute confidence in our relationship with God and a steadfast conviction in God's goodness and character. We place our hope in who God is, not in what we see (or do not see) in others. John's gospel tells us that "the Word became flesh and made his dwelling among us... full of grace and truth" (John 1:14). If God was fully human and dwelt among us full of grace and truth, then is it not possible for us to do the same? We do know that others are not perfect. That is easy to see. After all, we are all cracked pots, but we can also be full of grace, overlooking, ignoring, even forgiving the faulty behavior in others—just as God has done for us. To maintain hope in others begins with a firm conviction that it is possible to do so, and it is a choice that we make about how we are going to live. It starts with a resolve to be like Jesus, full of grace and truth. It is an act of faith.

When we resolve to maintain hope in others, it requires two qualities that are in short supply in our world: charity and trust. To behave with charity means to show tolerance, compassion, and generosity; to extend to others what we would want others to extend to us. It is a virtue that can be practiced, and we get better at it when we do. And along with charity, we can demonstrate trust—even to those who are not totally trustworthy. After all, that is all of us, isn't it? Trusting in those who are at times untrustworthy is surely an act of faith, maintaining hope without any assurance of the outcome. And, of course, at times we will be disappointed, even appearing to be silly or naïve, but our charity and trust are not dependent on how others behave. Instead, it is an expression of our faith in the God who extends the same to us. In doing so, our lives will demonstrate a certain dignity and sense of kindness in the world and toward the world. Maintaining hope in others, as it turns out, is good for us; it forms us even when others do not live up to our expectations and dreams for them. Maintaining hope in others is an act of faith, and it shapes the way we live our lives—and it shapes us, too.

If I were to sum up all that I have been trying to say in this portion of the chapter, it would be this: in the face of betrayal, deceit, meanness, and pain, we get to choose how we will live our lives. We get to choose how we see the world, and how we will make our way through it as we head for home. When we choose to keep vigil rather than dismiss others, to journey together rather than go it alone, and to maintain hope rather than cynicism despite the fact that we know that others will disappoint us from time to time, we are expressing a deep and formative faith in a God who did not give up on us. And at the end of the day, no matter how others have responded to the faith we have placed in them, we know that we have gone deeper in our own quest for holiness—to be like Jesus. We are on the journey home.

Scripture

Caleb

When I think about not losing faith in others, the story of Caleb quickly comes to mind (Num 13–14). You may recall that he was one of the twelve spies sent out by Moses on a reconnaissance mission to explore Canaan, assessing its agricultural possibilities and the strength of its defensive fortifications. Caleb returned full of optimism. He silenced the excited crowd and said, "We should go up and take possession of the land, for we can certainly do it" (Num 13:30). This, of course, was good news because the Israelites had been wandering in the desert for a very long time. However, most of the other spies were not so optimistic. In fact, they reported the presence of giants and "spread among the Israelites a bad report about the land they had explored. . . . We seemed like grasshoppers in our own eyes, and we looked the same to them" (Num 13:32–33). Grasshoppers, indeed. This was not good news. How would a bunch of wandering grasshoppers take on a formidable army in hostile territory? As a result of the majority report, the battle for Canaan was postponed and discord raged in the camps. Many even wanted to replace Moses with another leader who would take them back to, of all places, Egypt—back to bondage. What a dismal turn of events!

If anyone had the right to throw up their hands and walk away in disgust, it was Caleb—but he didn't. Instead, he kept vigil. He remained faithful to his people, to Moses, and to Moses' successor, Joshua. In fact, if we pick up the story forty-five years later, Joshua had just conquered Jericho and was in the process of dividing up the surrounding areas. Caleb comes to Joshua and reminds him about a piece of land in the hill country that Moses had promised the young spy those many years ago. Joshua remembers the promise, blesses Caleb, now eighty-five years old, and gives him his inheritance. The story ends with the land at rest from war (Num 14:6–15).

If there is a message to this story, I don't think it is that if you remain faithful, in the end you will get all that you have been promised. No, that's not why the story of Caleb is so important to us. Rather, the story illustrates that even in the face of bitter disappointment and frustration, it is possible to maintain faith in others, to keep vigil—even when they hold a different view of reality or intentionally work to undermine the hopes and dreams you carry. I don't think Caleb was at all happy about the circumstances and the events that unfolded in the ensuing years, but he lived with these people, his people, forty-five years before the vision he had when he returned from his spy mission became a reality—forty-five years! When we pray the prayer "For Today," asking God to help us get through another day and not lose faith in other people, Caleb can be a model and inspiration for us. I'm sure he prayed such a prayer himself on more than one occasion.

Peter

The Apostle Peter is one of my favorite figures in the Bible. He may have been named the rock, but he was certainly not a polished stone. He was rough, impetuous, and probably a bit headstrong, too. Right after Jesus feeds the five thousand (as told in all four gospels), the disciples get into a boat and start out for the other side of the lake. However, as the story goes, they were rowing directly into a stiff wind and making very little progress. Late that evening, they were still in the middle of the lake, worn out and ready to turn back, when Jesus walks by the boat. Of course, they are at first frightened, thinking that they are hallucinating or seeing a ghost, but according to the Gospel of Matthew, Jesus identifies himself, and Peter immediately wants to walk on water, too. So, he did, but as

Matthew tells it, Peter becomes frightened by the power of the waves and starts to sink. Jesus admonishes Peter for his lack of faith, fishes him out of the water, and they return to the boat. And when they do, the winds die down. The storm is over.

I have heard many sermons about Peter's bold faith and how we should trust Jesus when he tells us to come to him, and I certainly don't quibble with that message, but I think the story makes another point, perhaps the main point. To be clear, Luke does not report that Jesus walked on water at all, and Mark and John tell the story but there is no mention of Peter getting out of the boat (Mark 6:45–51; John 6:16–21). Only Matthew tells the story of Peter's walk on the water (Matt 14:22–33).

No one knows for sure why Mark and John didn't mention that Peter left the boat, but what is clear in all three gospel accounts is that the storm ceased and the winds died down when they were all back in the boat. Could it be that the point of the story is not so much about getting out of the boat but instead staying in it? To keep your oars in the water and stay together—the storms won't last? Could it be? I honestly think so. When we pray, "let me not lose faith in other people," even when rowing against a stiff wind, the solution may be staring us right in the face. Stay in the boat and row together.

Jacob

Jacob was traveling back to his ancestral home to meet up again with his older brother, Esau. They hadn't talked in years. When Jacob left home, fled actually, it was not under the best of circumstances. You see, Jacob tricked his father, Isaac, into giving him the blessing that belonged to his older brother. Esau vowed to kill Jacob as soon as their father died, and Isaac was in poor health. So, Jacob saw the writing on the wall and left to make a life for himself in Harran, and he did.

Now Jacob was coming home, and he was not certain whether he would be welcomed or killed on the spot. On the day before the meeting was to take place, he sent everyone on ahead of him—his wives, his children, and all the livestock. He stayed behind, ostensibly to pray. During that time alone, he surely remembered the promise that God made to him years earlier: "I am with you and will watch over you wherever you go, and I will bring you back to this land. I will not leave you until I have done what I have promised you" (Gen 28:15). Still, getting back home was one thing, staying alive was quite another.

That night, Jacob was visited by a man and they entered into an epic wrestling match. It lasted all night, and his hip was dislocated in the process. Still, Jacob would not let go until he received a blessing from the man. As it turns out, Jacob was wrestling with God. He did receive a blessing, including a new name, and at daybreak Jacob limped his way to his family and on to meet Esau. It turned out to be a happy reunion.

Jacob was a not a perfect person by any stretch of the imagination. He made his fair share of shady deals, but he had a promise from God, a covenant, that he held onto even when it hurt. He wouldn't let go until he received a blessing. The next morning, he limped off to meet his brother, not knowing what he would face. Like Jacob, I think we, all of us, have a covenant with God, too. God will be with us wherever we go; something we can hold on to even when it hurts. And like Jacob, we won't let go until we receive a blessing either. For me, this makes wrestling with God an act of faith. In fact, I believe that this striving *is* faith. We hold on as best we can in the middle of some very dark nights, and in the morning, we limp and lean into the challenges of each new day, praying to keep our faith in other people alive and fresh even as they limp along with us as best they can.

Some Practical Advice

Before we conclude this chapter on keeping our faith in others during difficult times, I want to share some words of practical advice. Honestly, none of these suggestions are earthshaking but I do believe that if taken seriously, they can be helpful to all of us as we navigate our way through choppy waters, striving to make our way safely home.

Forget Perfection

Say this with me: "Nobody's perfect." Now say it again: "Nobody's perfect—not even me." Deep down we know this to be true, yet some of us expect perfection from ourselves—an expectation that will lead to a sense of failure and regret. It's a setup. And many of us can be so critical of others, holding them to a much higher standard than we have for ourselves. That's a setup, too, and the disappointment we kindle and carry makes it easier to be dismissive of others.

Rather than insisting on perfection, focus instead on presence. Aspire to live justly, love mercy, and walk humbly with God (Mic 6:8), and be challenged to love God and neighbor with everything you have (Deut 6:5; Matt 22:37–39; Mark 12:30–31; Luke 10:27). And let others be present rather than perfect, too. It is the best way I know to maintain faith in others during difficult times.

Stay in the Boat

We learned from Peter that a walk on the water is tempting, but the storms cease when we all get back in the boat and Jesus joins us—working in our difficulties and teaching us through our difficulties. Of course, we all hope and pray for a miracle from time to time, and most of us enjoy being in the spotlight—even seek it out—but I have come to believe that most good things happen when we stay together, keeping our oars in the water, and our backs to the wind. Stay in the boat.

See a Portal, Not a Precipice

When we do have difficulties or disappointments with a friend or colleague, it is so easy to throw up our hands and wave them away. We write them off as if they fell off a cliff. Sadly, I've done it myself a time to two. It seems to me that it is much more helpful and graceful to think of such difficulties as a doorway or portal through which we step rather than a fall that ends the relationship. Surely, there may be necessary changes and new boundaries, but the intentional metaphor of a portal, not a precipice, gives grace and hope for a continuing journey together rather than the certain end of the relationship. I know that God has done the same with me on more than one occasion.

* * *

Before we conclude this chapter, there is one important caveat that must be made. In general, I do believe that maintaining our faith in others will require us to stay the course, keep vigil, and see our relationships with others as a portal rather than a precipice. However, there is a difference between swimming upstream, which will make you tired—and swimming up a toxic stream, which will make you sick. There are many spiritual practices and understandings to help you maintain your strength and integrity during difficult times, but if it is a toxic situation, you need to get out of the water. Hit the reset button and move on as best you can.

Conclusion

Faith, according to Hebrews, is confidence in what we hope for, an abiding assurance in what we do not see or cannot see—and maybe even in what we will never see. At times, our faith in others can be fleeting and fragile, particularly during difficulties. Our friends are not perfect. They will let us down, sometimes at the worst possible moment in the worst possible way. But if we are honest, we must confess that we have let others down on an occasion or two ourselves. After all, we are all broken pots. This is not an excuse; this is reality.

Yet, at the same time, our faith can be patient and persistent, a resolute assurance in seeing that which is invisible. We exercise our faith in others when we speak into their lives, expressing a hopeful confidence in who they are and who they might become—and when we allow others to speak into our circumstances and character, too. I believe these acts of faith in and with others are profound works of patience and grace. In difficult times, we pray that we will not lose faith in others. This is as it should be. If there is any hope for our shattered world, often shattered by our own doings, we really do need each other. Faith is the glue that holds us together as we journey homeward, limping along as best we can, holding on to the promise of a blessing. Together, we'll get there.

Questions for Reflection and Discussion

1. Why is it so easy for us to give up on others when they are less than perfect, even though we know that we are all imperfect and inconsistent? Is patience one of your virtues?
2. In this chapter, we read about keeping vigil, waiting and watching, as an act of faith. For whom or what are you keeping vigil? Is anyone keeping vigil for you?

3. Is it helpful to think about keeping faith in others as a long pilgrimage (journey) rather than an "in or out" proposition? As a portal rather than a precipice?

4. Of the three stories shared from Scripture—Caleb, Jacob, and Peter, with which story do you most identify? Why?

5. In what area of your life are you most tempted to walk on water rather than to stay in the boat? How can you best demonstrate your faith in others, particularly when going through difficulties?

For Today

O God:
Give me strength to live another day;
Let me not turn coward before its difficulties or prove recreant to its duties;
Let me not lose faith in other people . . .

5

Enduring Ingratitude, Treachery, and Meanness

> The ingratitude of the world can never deprive us of the conscious happiness of having acted with humanity ourselves.
>
> —OLIVER GOLDSMITH

Introduction

As a professor of management and an organizational consultant, I have had plenty of opportunities to observe healthy and unhealthy teams—and I've served on a few of each myself. I can tell you that a leadership team comprised of individuals with average to above-average talent can do amazing things when they pull together and cheer for each other. They can create an effective management team, empower their individual units to sing, and see the organization grow and develop. They can, that is, if gratitude, transparency, and kindness are an integral part of their work together. These virtues help ordinary teams to produce extraordinary results. They are the fuel that energizes the work and the glue that holds things together, particularly during difficult times. The same holds true for families, churches, not-for-profits, and organizations of all types, and in our personal lives, too. We all know that love covers over a multitude of sins (1 Pet 4:8); I believe that gratitude, transparency, and kindness do, too. They are the salve, the healing agents, in hurting organizations, family systems, and relationships.

However, we can all think of times when we have experienced ingratitude, treachery, and meanness in our work or in our personal relationships, or both. I know of an expert team, a leadership group with seasoned expertise in all positions, that was toxic and downright dysfunctional at times. They lacked the corporate ability to be thankful, honest, and gracious. These virtues were neither practiced nor welcomed. Being a part of such a team was, at best, frustrating and diminishing, and while many metrics and goals were achieved and celebrated, they were accomplished at a deep personal cost to many—and it was all so unnecessary.

At first, I thought the leader of this team had to be thankful for some things and pleased in some way, but simply didn't have the personal skills and know-how to express such feelings adequately, particularly in public. Many of us feel inadequate in expressing thankfulness from time to time. However, it was sobering to realize along the way that this leader did not express gratitude precisely because he was not grateful. It was not in his vocabulary because it was not part of his experience. His view was that everyone worked for him and should be happy just to have a job. His job was to be critical and demeaning, pointing out the flaws in everyone's work. Being grateful for the good work that was done simply didn't compute.

To compound this sad situation, the leader encouraged and delighted in his team members reporting things that other team members said or did that they thought counter to the direction of the organization or critical of his own leadership. It was a pitiful form of treachery, pitting one subordinate against the other, and being called into his office to explain a comment or decision (often taken completely out of context) promoted fear and uncertainty rather than honestly and trust.

And in addition to ingratitude and treachery, the leader was simply mean-spirited, not caring what his decisions did to those in the way, how it may upset their lives. Persons were fired without warning the week before Christmas in the name of right-sizing, annual contracts were altered without explanation—moving employees from full-time to part-time, or simply withheld or delayed for no particular reason, and privileges and perks were handed out or taken away at the whim of the leader like candy for children. Certainly, ingratitude, treachery, and meanness were a wicked trio, and while the organization looked impressive from the outside, many on the inside suffered unnecessarily and silently. Sad, indeed.

In this chapter, we will examine a powerful request from our daily prayer, "For Today": "Keep me sweet and sound of heart, in spite of ingratitude, treachery, and meanness." This is, indeed, an earnest and sometimes desperate prayer, and it is certainly only with God's grace and love that we can deal with such circumstances in a healthy fashion. So, how do we keep a sweet and sound spirit in the midst of such nasty experiences? To answer this question, we'll take a closer look at ingratitude, treachery, and meanness to see what is at work and what it means to endure them. Honestly, it is not easy. Then, we will offer some "next steps" to make our way from merely enduring to thriving, having "the conscious happiness of having acted with humanity ourselves." That is our prayer for today, and every day.

Enduring

Enduring is not necessarily the happiest of words. Honestly, we would just as soon have ingratitude, treachery, and meanness simply disappear or never experience them in the first place, but that isn't the way life works. Life is messy. When we pray, "Keep me sweet and sound of heart in spite of ingratitude, treachery, and meanness," it is an acknowledgment that some member of this disheartening trio will join us at some point on our journey—and perhaps we are dealing with one of them even now. Ultimately, our focus is how we can remain sweet and sound of heart in spite of such realities.

Ingratitude

Ingratitude is a package that comes in all sizes. Even though most of us were taught early in our childhood to say the magic words—please and thank you—it is troubling to see how many times adults fail to use them. The magic seems to be gone, and if we are honest it bothers us, perhaps more than it should but it bothers us nonetheless. We send a birthday gift and we do not receive a thank-you note or even an acknowledgment that the gift was received and appreciated. We take a meal to a family in distress or bereavement without receiving any word of appreciation. Sometimes we don't even get the dishes back. Or we go out of our way to do a favor for a friend or neighbor, and the act is treated more like an obligation than an act of generosity when a simple word of thanks would have sufficed. It bothers us.

Why? Why do these small acts of ingratitude go so against the grain? First, it is a matter of common courtesy. It is always appropriate to express gratitude when someone does something for you. However, some find it extremely difficult to do so. Perhaps gratitude has not been modeled for them and they are not sure what to say. Perhaps they are a very private person and cannot find the words to express their thankfulness. Perhaps they are so surprised or moved that words do not easily come. Perhaps they are embarrassed at receiving what they imagine to be an act of charity. And sometimes we don't receive the acknowledgment we expect because we expect too much. After all, did we prepare and deliver a meal to a friend in order to receive a welcome home parade? If so, there are easier ways to receive one.

Yet, there are times when we prepare a meal, send a gift, do a favor, or go out of our way to help a coworker, and there is no expression of gratitude because the person is so self-absorbed that it does not even occur to them to say thank you. Your act of generosity is expected, not coming out of kindness or concern, but as an obligation you owe them. They deserve it. They are takers. When you send your gift, you have just done your duty, so a thank you is neither necessary nor forthcoming. And if a gift is not sent, they are actually mad at you for ignoring them on their special occasion! Self-absorption and gratitude are like oil and water. They don't easily mix.

So, how do we endure acts of ingratitude? First, we remind ourselves that we do not do what we do to be appreciated, even while admitting that we receive a personal payoff when we are. That's human nature. We all want to find meaning in what we do, so a sincere expression of gratitude warms our hearts. It is okay to acknowledge that reality. We all want to be appreciated. However, if our own need for attention and appreciation drives our acts of compassion and generosity, the end result is certain. We will be sadly disappointed and probably hurt along the way.

We also need to be realistic about others, too. There are no guarantees that they will respond in the way that is meaningful to us, if at all. Giving without an expectation of a response is difficult, I admit, but possible. In fact, enduring ingratitude is easiest when we expect no overt response and are genuinely surprised and appreciative when our actions are acknowledged.

Finally, it is easier to endure ingratitude when we consciously remind ourselves that receiving no word of appreciation does not mean that our acts are unappreciated or without impact. In fact, most likely they are deeply appreciated—even if expressed years later. From time to time, I receive a note from a former student who writes to thank me for a conversation we had over lunch or a comment I made in class years ago. They tell me that they remember it clearly and it has shaped them in good ways. Honestly, I usually don't remember these comments and conversations at all—too much water under the bridge, I suppose, but they do! In the intervening years, the only thing I received was silence, but God was at work in their lives in ways that I could not even imagine. Enduring ingratitude is possible when we carefully examine our own motives and expectations, proceed with the understanding that we might not be recognized for what we do, and believe that regardless of the response we receive, we did the right thing by planting seeds that will bear good fruit in season.

Before we move on to discuss enduring treachery in our lives, one additional comment is in order. I have come to believe that expressing encouragement and appreciation are two things that cost nothing, but mean everything to those who need them—and that is all of us. Especially in work situations, it is easy for a supervisor or leader to simply assume that since everyone is getting paid, there is no need for expressions of appreciation. Wrong! Being appreciated is a way of being seen, and it is hurtful and debilitating to become invisible, particularly in the middle of a busy work setting. When you say "thank you," it is a way of saying, "I see you," and for most of us, it is just as important for our well-being as a raise in pay. And if this is true for paid staff, it is even more important for volunteers, the undergirding support system of many churches and not-for-profit organizations. A simple thank you can feed a volunteer's soul for weeks. Appreciation costs nothing, but means everything.

Treachery

Treachery is such a difficult thing to even discuss, let alone experience. We would like to think that betrayal, deceit, and dishonesty are the stuff of the movies, which they are, but sadly they are real, too. At some time or another, we will all come face-to-face with someone who is untrustworthy, who has an agenda, but it is not about our well-being. They may, in fact, appear to be quite friendly and supportive, but in the end their actions diminish, hurt, and embarrass. They may be friendly, but they are no friend.

At the heart of the matter, solid and supportive relationships must stand on a foundation of trust and honesty, but if someone does not have your best interests at heart, they undermine that foundation of trust, replacing it with bad intentions and hurtful outcomes. Certainly, if given even half a chance, we should avoid such situations like the plague, but the problem is that treachery is very difficult, if not impossible, to spot until we have been victimized by it. And once we realize that someone cannot be trusted, we do our best to minimize contact or at least keep all interchanges on a professional basis, sharing as little personal insights or feelings as possible. As my father would say, "If you don't want to be bitten by the dog, stay out of the kennel." This is good advice.

But what do you do if you simply cannot avoid the person; perhaps you are on a work team together and you realize that their intent is to embarrassed you, diminished your role, and ultimately oust you from the team? They don't like you and don't want you around. How do you endure such a situation? Honestly, there is no simple or satisfactory response to this level of treachery. Ultimately, one or the other will most likely have to go, because such a toxic situation is intolerable in the long run. You will not only become tired of it; it will make you sick. Short of hitting the reset button, however, there are several things you can do. First, be cordial but minimize your conversations about personal concerns. Don't share too much. In other words, don't give fodder for the fire. Second, have a frank conversation with that person, naming the difficulties at hand and seek to find a way to address them carefully and conscientiously. Of course, if they do not have your best interests at heart, they may deny that anything is actually going on or agree to just about anything. You have to remember that without trust, deceit is always a real possibility. Finally, talk to someone who is in a position to see and influence the situation, remembering all the while that if someone wants to make this a "win-lose" proposition, there is little you can do to prevent it—and you may well end up the loser.

Thankfully, I have only experienced such a scenario twice in my own career. The first experience was totally my fault. As a young administrator, I believed that my unit was more important than any other unit in the organization, and I said so publicly and acted that way in team meetings. Understandably, another vice president took exception and worked intentionally to undermine my role. We met over lunch and had a very frank and difficult conversation. In the end, I acknowledged my mistakes and apologized for my actions. We agreed that while we would probably not be the best of friends, we would support each other's work since we were both committed to the mission of the institution. The relationship was strained at times, never more than cordial, but not toxic. We made it work, and I learned a valuable lesson through the process.

The other situation was simply horrible. A colleague decided that my vision for the institution was patently misguided and simply wrong, characterizing it as an archaic view of the university that was no longer appropriate for the fast-paced world of business. In addition, he simply didn't like me and didn't want to be in relationship. Our conversations were measured and superficial, and it became clear to me that he was working at every turn to undermine my efforts and influence with our supervisor. When I spoke to our supervisor about the situation, he simply said that he had no intention to intervene but acknowledged that my colleague had his ear. The next week, I learned that one of my direct reports was working covertly with this colleague, making decisions that were mine to make. My boss knew about the end run and gave tacit approval to their actions. At that point, it was clear to me that I could not do my best work in such a situation. Faced with the prospects of backstabbing and betrayal, I saw no option other than to get out of the toxic stream. I negotiated a transition to another role in the organization, and I am so glad I hit the reset button when I did. The change was life-giving for me.

Sometimes you can endure treachery; sometimes you can't.

Meanness

I have nothing good to say about meanness on any level. Ingratitude, although frustrating, can be managed, and treachery, although damaging, can in some cases be held in check, but there is simply no place for meanness. At the heart of meanness, there is a lack of compassion and concern for people or the organization. Unkind, spiteful, selfish, and unfair behaviors kill the spirit. Health and hope are sacrificed when those with power are unwilling to give or share. It is a blatant form of baseless poverty. If meanness comes your way, and in the short run you have to endure it, what can you do? It takes real inner strength and courage to survive. One strategy is to minimize contact, giving as few opportunities to be treated spitefully as possible. Another strategy is to be mindful that this is ultimately not about you. Mean treatment often brings feelings of guilt and shame. Guilt is the feeling that you did something wrong, and shame is the feeling that something is wrong with you. We can easily be overwhelmed by such feelings and blame ourselves for the mistreatment. Remember, there is no excuse for being treated shabbily; it is not your fault. No one deserves to be treated that way. And finally, this is not a path you want to walk alone. It is critical that you have people in your life with whom you can share your hurt and have a good cry together. Meanness can be isolating and marginalizing. Stay together.

In the next section, we will examine ways to not only endure, but actually grow in the face of ingratitude, treachery and meanness—remaining sweet and sound of heart. Suffice it here to say that enduring disappointing and painful experiences is hurtful, but they can shape us and build character in good ways if we don't lose faith and direction. It isn't that we seek adversity in order to grow, but we do acknowledge that the God who is with us will prepare a table for us in the midst of our enemies (Ps 23:5). It is in the midst of the struggle that we pray that God will keep us sweet and sound of heart in spite of ingratitude, treachery, and meanness. As you will see, grace, hope, and healing abound.

Sweet and Sound of Heart

If possible, we, all of us, would avoid ingratitude, treachery, and meanness if we could, but life has a way of bringing both the good and the not-so-good our way. That's life. It's messy. But like David, I can attest that we are not left entirely to our own wits when adversity calls. God does prepare a table for us in the midst of our enemies. Think about that picture for just a minute. It the middle of nasty and hurtful situations, a table is set for us and a banquet is served. This is an amazingly comforting picture. The battle rages around us, but we sit down to a feast. In the midst of ingratitude, treachery, and meanness, we can remain sweet and sound of heart.

We know that we grow through adversity. These times can shape us in healthy ways, challenging us to go deeper, hold tighter, and rely more on others. In the process, we learn more about God's grace and about the goodness of others. We can become more attuned to the pain and alienation around us, hearing and seeing our neighbors as never before.

Even though we cannot choose what happens to us, we can choose how we respond. As we pray to be kept sweet and sound of heart, is there a part for us to play? The answer is, of course, yes. Here are several strategies during particularly dark days as we pray to remain sweet and sound of heart.

Manage to Minimize

That is, in the midst of these difficulties, manage your day in order to minimize contact and exposure to hurtful situations and people. Be intentional about staying clear of nasty situations when you can. Choose your battles carefully.

Avoid Negative Self-Talk

It is so easy to lose confidence in yourself and even in your calling when faced with meanness and treachery. Believe in yourself, your gifts and graces, and don't let anyone take away your confidence. They can't if you do not let them. Don't blame yourself for what others do to you.

Stay Visible and Active

The temptation in the face of adversity is to hide, to stay home and not show your face in public. That is a huge mistake. Isolation breeds negative self-talk and minimizes opportunities for others to speak into your situation. Get out of bed, wash your face, and get out and go about your business. Even a walk around the neighborhood is a step in the right direction.

Undertake Some Life-Giving Activities

Instead of going into hibernation, which is a real temptation, think instead about what gives you energy and fills your soul. It could be working with wood, preparing a meal for a family in need, playing music, hiking in the redwoods, writing a book, taking a course, learning a new craft, or reading the Bible. The key is to remember that difficulties can sap your energy, physically and spiritually, so finding ways to refill your cup are essential. It is difficult to survive, let alone serve and grow, when your cup is empty.

Choose to Grow

Ultimately, even in dark and difficult times, there are things within our control—choices we can make. These choices will not make our own difficulties go away, but in the face of ingratitude, we can choose to be gracious. In the face of treachery, we can choose to be open and honest. And in the face of meanness, we can choose to treat others with dignity, kindness, and respect. When we pray, asking God to keep us sweet and sound of heart in spite of ingratitude, treachery, and meanness, we acknowledge that we will not be rescued from our difficulties, as nice as that would be. They simply won't go away. Rather, we have a banquet table set for us in the midst of our difficulties and dark times, and God bids us to come and dine. The battles may rage, but we have sustenance and fellowship as we make our way. Our prayer is not merely to endure, although on some days I admit that that is all you can do, but to flourish, to center, to go deep—remaining sweet and sound of heart in spite of the negativity that comes our way.

Scripture

I want to look at three stories from Scripture that deal in one way or another with ingratitude, treachery, or meanness. There is much wisdom to be mined from them, lessons for each one of us. Although we are not the original subjects of these stories, we can locate ourselves in them. Truly, in a deeply significant way, they were written about us and for us.

The Ten Lepers: Ingratitude

Luke tells an interesting story of the healing of ten lepers (Luke 17:11–19). Jesus is on his way to Jerusalem, traveling along the border between Galilee and Samaria. Galileans didn't have much to do with Samaritans if given half a chance. Ten lepers stood at a distance (because they were deemed unclean and social outcasts), crying out for mercy. Luke tells what happened next: "When he saw them, he said, 'Go show yourselves to the priests.' And as they went, they were cleansed. One of them, when he saw he was healed, came back, praising God in a loud voice. He threw himself at Jesus' feet and thanked him—and he was a Samaritan" (Luke 17:14–16). Jesus took note that while there were ten lepers who were healed, only one, "this foreigner," returned to express gratitude and give praise to God. Then, Jesus sent him on his way, noting that his faith had made him well, and as far as we know Jesus went on his way, too.

What an interesting story. There is no mention of what happened to the other nine lepers. When they showed themselves to the priest, were they still in good health? It is likely that they were, but we do not know. We do know that it made sense to send them to the priest because they were social and religious outcasts. The priest could inspect them and begin the process by which they would be pronounced ceremonially clean and able to take part in the community of faith once again. We do not know how many of the lepers were Samaritans—maybe only one. Showing himself to the priest would certainly have been more problematic. Perhaps he was an outcast in a group of outcasts—the worst of the worst. We do not know. But we do know this: only this one returned to give thanks, and we read about his gratitude two thousand years later.

I think we can take three things from this story. First, Jesus took note that only one of the ten returned to express gratitude. I seriously doubt that it took him by surprise. My view is that he made a point of it to highlight that even in the most amazing and miraculous circumstances, people don't often stop and say thank you. They just don't. In Jesus' own experience, it was 10 percent. You set yourself up for disappointment if you expect a higher rate of return.

Second, the leper who did return and give thanks received a blessing. I don't think this means that if we express gratitude, God will give each of us a special blessing, but I do think it is fair to say that when we express gratitude, something happens to us, in us. We are shaped and formed by our own expressions of gratitude. When we stop, go back and say thank you, we acknowledge the work of God in and through others, and it changes us in profound ways.

Finally, after Jesus noted that many did not return to say that they were grateful, he went on his way, continuing his journey to Jerusalem. He didn't hunt down the nine to give them a lecture, punish them, or take back his healing act of compassion. No, he did what he did, blessed the one who returned, and then continued on his way. He didn't let ingratitude deter or disrupt him from his mission.

These are powerful lessons for all of us who pray that we remain sweet and sound of heart in spite of ingratitude.

Judas: Treachery

The story of Judas Iscariot is told in all four gospels. It is certainly a sad story. Here is Judas, one of the twelve disciples, part of the inner circle, who would betray Jesus, playing a part in sending Jesus to the cross. His name is synonymous with treachery. No one names their son Judas. Did he play this part willingly? Did he have a choice? Was he simply swept away by the events of the times or was this a role he was destined or predestined to play? Of course, there are no clear and satisfying answers to these questions, and the arguments about Judas' role continue to the present day. I will humbly confess that if there are any definitive answers, I do not have them. But I do know that, at the very least, Jesus surely expected that treachery could be afoot. After all, he read human nature better than any of us, and he was predicting his own demise. Yet, he kept his disciples close: washing their feet, breaking bread together, and encouraging and praying with them and for them—trusting even while knowing that they would not always make good choices. None of us do.

Why? Why would Jesus do this in the face of treachery, disloyalty that could lead to his own death? My view is that Jesus was giving Judas every benefit of the doubt, hoping beyond hope that he was wrong about him, praying that he would make good choices. Of course, in the end Judas did not, and it cost everyone dearly.

So, what can we take from this story? I don't think the takeaway is that treachery is something that died with Judas and we should go through life believing that everyone has our best interests at heart. No, deceit, disloyalty, and betrayal show up in the most sacred places, our homes, our churches, our workplaces, and our neighborhoods. Being a Christian is no insurance policy against such nastiness. Life is messy to be sure. But we do have a choice in how we live our lives. At some cost, we can go through life holding everything close to the vest, trusting no one, protecting ourselves as best we can from any possibility of being betrayed, or we can embrace life with open arms, knowing that there will be those who will not have our best interests at heart—and at some point, we will most likely be hurt. We might also look foolish and naïve, but it is a choice we can make, a choice to be sweet and sound of heart in spite of treachery. We can't ultimately determine how others will treat us, but we can choose how we will live in the face of such treatment. For me, I want to give those around me the benefit of the doubt—washing their feet, breaking bread together, providing encouragement, praying for reconciliation, and hoping that good choices are made. Of course, the outcomes are beyond my control, but to be honest, so is much of life. I choose to be a faithful presence where I am planted, joining David at the feast in the midst of my enemies. I encourage you to do the same.

King Herod: Treachery & Meanness

The story of the birth of Jesus in Bethlehem is found in Matthew and Luke, but only Matthew includes the visit and gifts of the magi and the treachery and meanness of King Herod (Matt 2:1–18). The arrival of the magi in Jerusalem who were looking for the baby king of the Jews gave the local religious establishment and the Roman government quite a jolt, especially King Herod. No despot wants to hear about any potential competition. He called a secret meeting with the magi to learn the whereabouts of the baby king, and asked them to return to Jerusalem after they had found the baby and tell him the baby's location so he could go and worship the newborn king, too. Of course, that was a lie and the magi saw through his ploy. They returned home by another way, which made Herod frightfully angry. As a result, Herod ordered that all boys younger than two years old in and around Bethlehem should be killed, eliminating all prospects of competition. However, Joseph, Mary, and the baby were already on the road to Egypt before the troops arrived in Bethlehem. In many respects, the story of the birth of Jesus is the most wonderful and the most tragic of all time, all at the same time.

What can we learn from the magi in the face of treachery and meanness? Let me offer three takeaways. First, Herod called a secret meeting with the magi. Beware of secret meetings! Of course, there are some good reasons for meeting privately, but my experience is that when you are asked to meet in secret, something is up—and it is not always what it appears to be. Be careful. Second, at the meeting Herod lied to the magi, asking them to reveal Jesus' location so he could come and worship, too. Instead, it would have been the Roman troops that arrived with swords, not gifts. The magi saw through the ruse and headed home by another way. It is always important to be clear about what is being asked of you, particularly in secret, and when asked to be complicit in treachery, do everything you can to avoid it, even if it makes someone mad at you. Make your way home by another way.

Finally, in spite of your best efforts, there may be horrific pain and suffering accompanying even the best of events. That's a part of the story that is not often brought up at Christmas Eve celebrations, but it is part of life, too. When someone is mean, someone gets hurt. Remaining sound of heart requires vigilance and insight in the face of treachery and meanness, and a resolute conviction to avoid or mitigate them as best we can as we reach out to those who are wounded in its wake. When someone is hurt, we are all diminished.

Some Practical Advice

This chapter is salted throughout with practical advice, so I will try here to be brief and avoid being repetitive or redundant. There are two relevant words of wisdom from Proverbs that I want to share with you. The first is this: "The prudent *see danger and take refuge*, but the simple keep going and pay the penalty" (Prov 22:3). There are two actions here—seeing danger and taking refuge. I surely do not want us to be paranoid about our circumstances, but it is wise, I think, to be mindful that meanness and treachery can lurk in the most unassuming places, including Christian organizations. So, don't be paranoid but be mindful, vigilant, and if you witness or experience treachery or meanness, take refuge. That is, take the necessary measures to protect yourself and others, and don't just push blindly forward, wishing and hoping that everything will work out for the better. Usually, they do not.

Second, the best antidote to ingratitude, treachery, and meanness is to practice generosity, honesty, and kindness. In doing so, you will be an encouragement to others. Proverbs puts it this way: "A generous person will prosper; whoever refreshes others will be refreshed" (Prov 11:25). As we are gracious, we are refreshed. As we live honestly and openly, we are refreshed. And as we are kind and generous, we are refreshed. We are shaped and formed in good and healthy ways when we focus on the needs of others. It is so true that in giving, we also receive.

Finally, how do we keep our attention on remaining sweet and sound of heart instead of focusing on the ingratitude, treachery, and meanness around us? Micah 6:8 tells us that in the face of injustice, we are to act justly. In the face of intolerance, we are to love mercy. And in the face of hubris, we are to walk humbly with our God. This is good advice for all of us. When we are intentional about justice, mercy, and humility, our spirits are refreshed, and we provide hope to those around us, too

Conclusion

In this chapter, we examined this line from our daily prayer, "For Today": "Keep me sweet and sound of heart in spite of ingratitude, treachery, and meanness." After looking at some reasons why ingratitude, treachery, and meanness persist and some ways to address or minimize their impact on our lives, we turned our attention to the first part of the prayer—keep me sweet and sound of heart. It is important to keep the main thing the main thing. Our focus is on remaining sweet and sound of heart, returning good for evil. While we cannot control what happens to us, we can choose how we will respond when we are treated in hurtful ways. The best antidote for shabby treatment is to be determined to live justly, love mercy, and walk humbly with God. Doing so will not make all our difficulties simply go away. But in the midst of the difficulties, we will find a table set for us—and God bids us to come and dine. In spite of ingratitude, treachery, and meanness, we can be shaped and formed in good and humane ways, and we can be a cup of strength to others, too. That is our prayer for today.

Questions for Reflection and Discussion

1. Think of a time when someone said "thank you" or showed their appreciation to you in a unique and personal way. How could you practice it forward?

2. Think of activities, places, and relationships that give you energy and fill your spirit. Do you revisit these life-giving activities regularly, especially during difficult times? Could you make a "fill my cup" list and keep it in a place where it will serve as a regular reminder?

3. What strategies can you use or have you used to minimize and protect yourself when you must deal with those who are untrustworthy or simply mean?

4. As you look back, how have you grown from experiences of ingratitude, treachery, or meanness?

5. How do you distinguish between a difficult and a toxic situation? In other words, how would you know when it is time to hit the reset button and move on?

FOR TODAY

O God:
Give me strength to live another day;
Let me not turn coward before its difficulties or prove recreant to its duties;
Let me not lose faith in other people;
Keep me sweet and sound of heart in spite of ingratitude, treachery, and meanness . . .

6

Minding and Giving Little Stings

> Bees cannot sting and make honey at the same time. They have to make a choice. Either they are going to be a stinger or a honey-maker.
>
> —EMANUEL CLEAVER

> Kindness in ourselves is the honey that blunts the sting of unkindness in another.
>
> —WALTER SAVAGE LANDON

Introduction

Part 1 of this book, "In the Ditch," ends with this chapter—minding and giving little stings. Thus far, we have been examining some of the negativity that rears its ugly head when we face difficult times, and sadly during some ordinary times, too. When we're in the ditch, it is so easy to lose our focus, our strength, our courage, our motivation, and even our faith in other people. And it is not easy to remain sweet and sound of heart in the face of ingratitude, treachery, and meanness. These realities can certainly take their toll on body and spirit, but as we saw in the last chapter, it is possible to manage and minimize them, and more importantly, to rise above them and to learn from them. When we're in the ditch, life certainly gets messy, but we know that God is faithful and in the ditch with us, bringing grace, hope, and healing, a veritable banquet set for us in the midst of these enemies.

In part 2, "On Down the Road," we will look at spiritual steps for moving beyond our difficult times, getting out of the ditch and heading on down the road—and helping others to do the same. It is energizing and inspiring to look forward with a renewed sense of the journey, traveling with a new vision and a vital spirit of joy and gladness. All of this we will cover in part 2, but first there is one more aspect of negativity that comes our way during difficult times, minding and giving little stings, what I call the mosquito bites of life. No one sting is as traumatic or devastating as treachery or meanness, but a swarm of mosquitoes can drive you out of the woods—or out of a job or a relationship. And far too often, if we are not mindful, we'll sting those around us, too.

In this chapter, we will give our attention to a profound line from our daily prayer, "For Today": "Preserve me from minding little stings or giving them." We'll first look at the nature of little stings and why they hurt us so much. Then, we'll explore constructive ways to deal with them when they come, and how to refrain from giving them back when they do. Hopefully, we can produce honey, not more stings.

Before we get into this chapter, however, I want to share three short vignettes, each about a different type of little sting—teasing, criticism, and slights. Whoever came up with the old saying that "stick and stones may break my bones, but words can never harm me" (first recorded in 1862) obviously lived a very insular life or had a faulty memory, or both. Little stings can certainly leave their mark.

Vignette One: Teasing

Growing up, I had a most favorite uncle and a least favorite uncle. My most favorite uncle lived next door to us, and he was always willing to come out and play with us in the yard. He teased us all the time, especially when we played backyard baseball. It was a good-natured ribbing, of course, and we, each of us, were kind of pleased when he called us out by name, usually for a poor throw or for turning our heads when we tried to short-hop the ball at first base. He called it an Arlie Latham. "Don't do an Arlie Latham, Patrick!" he would shout, or, "Come on, Arlie, keep your eye on the ball next time. Don't turn your head!" We would grin and try harder. We knew that he was trying to teach us some valuable skills to make us better baseball players, and he did it was a smile and a laugh that was contagious. It was fun to play with our favorite uncle, and we became better players, too. He teased us, but in ways that were somehow both kind and gentle. He brought out our best efforts, and we couldn't wait for the next backyard derby. Decades later, I discovered that Arlie Latham was a major-league baseball player in the early 1900s. I have one of his baseball cards displayed on my desk as a remembrance of my favorite uncle. He is gone, and I wish he could tease me even now.

My least favorite uncle would tease us, too, but it wasn't a game by any measure. He would call attention to us in the middle of a family gathering, pointing out something we were wearing, or our haircuts, or the quality of our shoes. He would make fun of us any time he could, but he never really talked to us—only about us and in front of others. It was absolutely painful. It was obvious that he was trying to embarrass us without any real purpose that we could imagine. We avoided his attention like the plague. He was no fun to be around, and to be honest I don't have any remembrances of him on my desk. There is simply no relationship to commemorate.

Two uncles, both teasers, but one made honey while the other only stung.

Vignette Two: Criticism

Sports has always been a huge part of my life. As a young boy, I dreamed of being a major leaguer in baseball and basketball at the same time, like Dave DeBusschere, who played with the Chicago White Sox (MLB) and the Detroit Pistons (NBA). As it turned out, however, I didn't have the talent and ability for either, but I loved to play nonetheless, and did so in high school and college.

I suppose that many players have a love-hate relationship with their coaches. In my case, it was really one or the other. One of my coaches was a stern taskmaster, never shy about yelling and correcting his players, including me, in practice or in a game. If you didn't run the offense correctly or were out of position on defense, you heard about it in no uncertain terms. He would call you out and correct you on the spot, yet deep down we knew that it was for the betterment of the team, and we knew that he cared deeply for each of us. He wanted the best for us.

The other coach I have in mind was not shy about criticism either. He would almost go ballistic with anger while dressing down a player, especially in public. His face would go red and his veins would pop. He would stare, scream, curse, wave his arms, point his finger, and criticize, and then escort the offending player to the bench where the tirade would continue for what seemed an eternity. The player was humiliated, and all of us were embarrassed for both of them. I was the captain of the team. On more than one occasion, I intervened, telling the coach that the team would walk off the floor if he didn't calm down, and on one occasion, we would not take the floor for the second half until he regained his senses. It was an ugly scene.

So, what was the difference? While both coaches corrected and criticized us, one was kind; one was not. We had a healthy relationship with one; the other we only endured. We respected and admired one coach; there was nothing to respect or admire in the other's behavior. We knew that one coach loved us; the other coach had no familiarity with the word. One coach surely wanted to win but he treated his players with dignity and respect; the other coach only cared about his record. We would run through a wall for one coach if he asked us to. We would run through a wall to avoid the other. Without kindness and respect, each criticism stung like a bee.

Vignette Three: Exclusion

Realizing you've been left out or off the invitation list is never a picnic. I remember coming home one afternoon from middle school. In our little town, no one had fences so it was easy to see what was going on at the neighbors. On the next street over, there was a big birthday party going on in our neighbor's backyard, complete with balloons, music, games, presents, and cake. One of my good friends lived there, and I was stunned to see most of my classmates playing in the backyard. For the life of me, I couldn't understand why I wasn't invited. Honestly, I still can't. It really stung. In middle school, all you want to do is fit in, and I was definitely out. As I shed some tears, my mom tried to console me: "They probably just forgot or the post office delivered the invitation to the wrong address. I'm sure it was just a mistake." There's really not much you can do with such a sting other than go about your business and be mindful of the potential of delivering little stings whenever you write out an invitation list yourself.

I also remember an exclusion that stings to this day, even though I was long past middle school. At the university where I worked, I had two very close friends. We would meet every other Friday at a local German restaurant, tell stories and laugh while we downed the locally made bratwurst. We were good friends, and our conversations were rich and real. I wouldn't miss a lunch to meet with the mayor of the city. For me, these were sacred times.

Sacred, that is, until I announced that I had accepted a job at another university and would be leaving in a few months. Something changed. When I emailed my buddies to nail down the time to meet for our next lunch, I received no reply. So just before lunch time, I called one of the friends. When he answered, he sounded sheepish and a bit apologetic: "Well, I think we have other plans today. Maybe next time." Next time? I didn't know what that meant or how to respond, so I simply said that I would look forward to it—the next time. My office was positioned near the university's front gate, so I could see any vehicle entering and leaving campus. I was sitting at my desk when I saw my friends drive off the campus, and there was someone else in the back seat, sitting in my place. They were off to the German restaurant without me.

It was a little sting. For whatever reason, I had been excluded from the lunch, and deep down I realized that there would not be a next time, and I was right. Not only was I excluded; I had been replaced. That was a double sting.

Being left out is a difficult sting to mind at any age.

*　*　*

I share these vignettes to offer some context for the discussion that follows. We'll look first at the nature of little stings, how to best navigate them when they come, and how we can refrain from returning them when they do, although I must admit that I have been seriously tempted to do so on more than one occasion. When we sincerely ask God to preserve us from minding little stings or giving them, it is a prayer that requires each of us to do some earnest inner work, too, if we want to get out of the ditch and on down the road.

Stings

Little stings come in all shapes and sizes, and from all directions, too. Sometimes they are innocently delivered, isolated events, but at other times they are intentionally given, and their impact is cumulative. Repeatedly being stung can wear you out physically, emotionally, and spiritually. While it is possible to wave away a solitary mosquito, dealing with a swarm is a different matter altogether.

Words

Let's talk first about words. Words matter. I first heard this phrase as a young university faculty member. At a faculty meeting early in my first year of service, there was a good-natured give-and-take among the faculty, and I joined in with a quip at someone's expense that brought the house down with laughter. While we all laughed, however, he sat there with a red face. I had called him out and he was embarrassed. After the meeting, a senior faculty member came to my office and reminded me that faculty members take words seriously, and we are all obligated to use them carefully—and never at someone's expense. It was a lesson well-learned. To this day, I have been careful how I use my words in public or in private. And I've learned along the way that it isn't just university faculty who take words seriously, we all do. Words can inspire, uplift, and encourage, and they can demean, embarrass, and humiliate. Words matter.

I believe words matter because they have power to persist. When spoken, hurtful language doesn't just disappear into thin air. No, like seeds in soil, they take root, sprout, and bear fruit. Our words take us somewhere, having a moral trajectory of their own, and we can't always anticipate where they will go or what will become of them. And we just can't simply take them back once they are out. They represent who we are for good or for ill. As it turns out, what is in the heart is made evident by what we say.

In one sense, words are free, but they can come with a real cost. Words can sting. They can break a heart, instantly ruin an entirely good day, or completely change one's attitude and outlook. With words, we can criticize, tease, belittle, judge, disapprove, slight, and embarrass. Even little jokes and pranks can sting, and they can't be simply explained away by offering that "we were only joking." In the end, little things that embarrass, hurt, humiliate, harden, and belittle are no joking matter in any sense of the word.

There is good reason why we are cautioned in Scripture over one hundred times about using our tongues (and words) in hurtful ways. The tongue is characterized as a burning fire, a poison, a wild animal, and a sword, all of which can bring pain and introduce uncertainty. What is certain, of course, is that words matter.

Deeds

Words matter, and our actions often speak louder than our words, and can carry a mean sting, too. I want us to look at some stings that can take a heavy toll on our relationships at work, in the home, and at church, and with our self-esteem, too. The first type of sting is what I call an act of privilege—moving to the front of the line, sitting at the head table, taking center stage, grabbing the best perks, vacation schedule, or office location, or having the first and best phone upgrade. The simple message is that you are less important than they, and they don't mind you knowing it. It is status and position power on display. I suppose that there's always a bit of chicken fighting that goes on in any organization to align status with rewards, but when there is a consistent pattern of others getting first dibs and you ending up with the leftovers, the message is clear—and it stings.

A second two-edged sting has to do with behaviors related to giving and taking credit. More precisely, the stings that come when credit is not given when due and when someone else takes credit for your work. I know of a very talented and dedicated academic team who toiled all summer to prepare for a special accreditation visit. They were seeking approval to start a new doctoral program, and failing to do so would have serious implications for the institution's budget, and repercussions for their jobs, too. They worked at a furious pace all through the summer. Vacations and special family activities were postponed or foregone altogether, and most weekends were spent working on the project. When the visiting team finally arrived, the team was ready and sailed through the review with flying colors. It was a most celebratory and gratifying day. Celebratory, that is, until the university actually scheduled a celebration event later that afternoon, summoning all available faculty and staff to come and celebrate together. Imagine the sting when the university leader failed to acknowledge all the time and effort given by the team over the summer, and took the lion's share of the credit for himself, explaining that when he met with the accreditation team, he offered them some very good local wine, and that, in his mind, made all the difference! Not giving credit and taking undue credit stings, and such needless stings are not easily forgotten.

Another sting involves withholding approval or praise. Expressing appreciation and giving recognition for a job well done cost virtually nothing, but these acts mean so much to the recipient. Someone who cannot or will not express appreciation misses an opportunity to give honey rather than a well-placed sting. Saying "I'm proud of you" and "you did a good job" can inspire and motivate for months, and it is so easy to do. Sadly, being ignored can sting for months, too. Purposely withholding approval is the practice of small individuals who lack the ability to be gracious, who try to build themselves up by putting everyone else down. Certainly, constant criticism and belittling can kill your self-confidence a little at a time; being ignored and made invisible can, too. The stings are cumulative.

One final sting bears mentioning—embarrassment. Being called out or set up for failure or purposely embarrassed is hurtful and humiliating. I remember enduring the middle school years. My friends and I would walk around together like a school of fish, hoping to blend together and not call undue attention to ourselves. I just wanted to fit in and not be embarrassed. It didn't happen very often, but when it did it was a terribly painful experience. Middle school is not easy on one's self-esteem. Now, some fifty years later, I can be a bit more mature and philosophical about being embarrassed, but I still avoid situations where that might occur like the plague. Being embarrassed stings most of us at any age and the stings heal slowly. And when the stings are intentional, it is indeed toxic. I guess these stings hurt so badly because they cut to the very core of our self-esteem, our well-being. It only takes one or two and we're headed out of the woods on a dead run.

Silence

Before we move on to a discussion of how we might manage little stings and stay out of the business of returning them, I want us to consider one additional kind of sting that many of us face far too often, and practice from time to time ourselves. While words matter and actions often speak louder than words, silence can have a language and sting of its own. Of course, silence can be good, helpful, even golden, but it can also be hurtful, especially when it is used to express disapproval, disappointment, judgment, or exclusion. Many family systems have developed the use of silence into an art form: a shake of the head that signals disappointment, a disapproving huff, stare, or snicker, or a cold shoulder that makes someone feel unimportant, unnecessary, even invisible.

I vividly remember my last at-bat my freshman year in high school. I was on the junior varsity baseball team, and was inserted as a pinch hitter with the bases loaded and two outs in the ninth inning. We were trailing by one run. Of course, I had visions of hitting a solid single to left field and driving in the game-winning runs. When the count became full (three balls and two strikes), I heard my dad yell from behind the backstop, "Come on, Patrick!" I so much wanted to make him proud of me. Unfortunately, I took the next pitch and was called out on strikes, thus ending the game. I immediately looked back at my father. He looked directly at me for just a moment, and when our eyes met he slowly turned around and walked to his truck. We never talked about that little sting, and in some sad way, I still feel like a failure every time I think about it. I honestly do not know what he was thinking or feeling at the time, but his silence spoke volumes to me.

Although the painful use of silence often originates in the family of origin, it is easily carried over and practiced in our schools, workplaces, churches, and communities. Sadly, this type of silence is far too prevalent, even acceptable, in our day-to-day lives. We look askance at tight-knit communities who shun and expel their own, but in so many ways, we practice small doses of this cold-blooded silence ourselves. Such behavior brings no honey, only stings.

Not Minding and Giving Little Stings

When all is said and done, we can't avoid little stings any more than we can avoid ants at a picnic. If we spend any time at all with others, a sting or two will come our way, and more than likely, we'll sting a friend or colleague, too. Such is life. Stings cannot be totally avoided. And the reality is that stings hurt the most when delivered by those we love, admire, and respect.

So, what part do we play when we ask God to preserve us from minding little stings and giving them? I think we start by being honest with reality. No one is perfect, not even those who love us the most, so from time to time we'll get stung. But such stings are not lethal; they hurt but they won't kill us. Of course, it is prudent to manage both their frequency and their impact. Often, a quick face-to-face conversation can nip the behavior in the bud. In any case, don't let the possibility of a sting keep you out of the clover. Also, it is always helpful to keep some perspective about what and why such stings are happening. Talk to a close friend or spiritual advisor about the impact such stings are having on you, what you might learn from them, and how to directly confront them if necessary.

Hopefully, the strategies just mentioned are both practical and helpful; however, I want to discuss something that by the standards of this world will be judged to be naïve or just plain crazy. If we earnestly ask God to preserve us from minding or giving little stings, it will take some serious and intentional spiritual work on our part. First, we ask God each day to help us be mindful of grace, his grace, and to live gracefully. God didn't let our sins and failures stand in the way of a relationship with him, and I believe that we can extend grace, too, giving others the benefit of the doubt and extending outright forgiveness. What if we made grace-giving the fundamental purpose for each day? I know this is a serious and challenging spiritual act, but I truly believe that we can do so with God's help. Could it be that we are called to live in an attitude of forgiveness, even as the bees swarm? This, it seems to me, can only be done with and in God's grace as we strive to live faithfully in a world that we know full well will come at us from time to time with mean intent.

If we started out each day by asking God to help us be kind persons, to give the benefit of the doubt, and a second chance whenever possible, couldn't we make honey instead of promoting anger, bitterness, and retribution? I believe it is a choice we can make, an intentional spiritual act, to be the honey that blunts the sting of unkindness in others. I readily admit that this is a daunting way to embrace our world, but with God's help I believe that we can faithfully live it out. It is a compelling way to love God and neighbor with all our hearts. Let honey flow.

Scripture

In the last chapter, we looked at a number of intimidating and hurtful difficulties, sobering things, bigger things like ingratitude, treachery, and meanness. In this chapter, we have been discussing smaller irritations, little stings, and praying for help to neither mind nor return them. I want us to look at three instances in the life of Jesus where his work and intentions were misunderstood. Of course, he faced enormous difficulties, even death, so these were relatively little stings, but stings nonetheless. I believe we, all of us, can learn from his responses. As it turns out, grace and compassion were the order of the day.

A Question from John the Baptist

No one knows for sure why John the Baptist sent two of his followers to question Jesus about his activities, but send them he did (Luke 7:18–26). John was sitting in Herod's prison, his own future quite uncertain. No doubt that he was alone, afraid, and discouraged, and perhaps disillusioned, but why did he worry about Jesus? Did he have doubts about Jesus being the messiah? Was he worried that he had prepared the way for the wrong person? Was he concerned that Jesus was going about his mission all wrong? Was Jesus too passive? Did he want to see more action? We do not know, of course, but we do know that John's two disciples came to Jesus early in his ministry and on behest of John asked this question, "Are you the one who is to come, or should we expect someone else?" (Luke 7:19). Wow, what a tough question, a sting to be sure.

It seems to me that Jesus had every reason and right to be indignant. After all, wasn't John's mother, Elizabeth, one of the first to know of Jesus' coming birth? Didn't Mary and Elizabeth spend months together? Didn't they talk about the visit of the angel? Wasn't John's father visited by an angel, too? And didn't John baptize Jesus in the Jordan River, seeing the spirit descend upon him like a dove and hearing the voice of God affirm his identity? Did he forget all their history, all that they had been through together?

Jesus could have easily and understandably given John's disciples a piece of his mind and sent them away. After all, they were questioning not only his calling and his ministry, but also his very identity—and doing so in public. It could have been an ugly scene, but it wasn't. Rather, Jesus told his questioners to go back to John and report what they had witnessed: the blind receiving their sight, the lame walking . . . and good news preached to the poor (Luke 7:22). Surely, John would have recognized that this response had the fingerprints of the prophet Isaiah all over it, and he would have been satisfied. That could have been the end of the confrontation, turned away with a kind and hopeful response, but that wasn't the end. Jesus then turned to the crowd of listeners and talked to them about John the Baptist, the one who had just questioned his ministry, or at least his tactics as the coming messiah. He praised and affirmed John, telling them that he was a prophet and a good one, and much more. He was a forerunner, and one of the best persons he knew. Instead of giving back a little sting, he affirmed and honored instead. To me, that is grace in action.

A Mother's Request

In this story, Jesus is going about the region preaching to large crowds and teaching his disciples. At a particularly poignant moment on the way to Jerusalem, he takes his twelve disciples aside and tells them for a third time that he would be crucified there (Matt 20:17–19). Obviously, he wanted his closest disciples to be clear about his mission and the path he was about to take. What happens next is quite unexpected in one respect, but so very human in another. The mother of James and John, two of his closest disciples, comes and kneels before Jesus to ask if her two sons could have preferred seating, one on his left and one on his right, when he enters his kingdom (Matt 20:20–28). They were asking to have places of honor. What a sting, and on so many levels.

First, how could these trusted disciples so misunderstand the nature of his kingdom? Had they not been listening when he taught about who would be greatest in the kingdom of heaven, or about the unmerciful servant or the workers in the vineyard? Did they just not get it? And second, to have their mother come and do the asking added insult to injury. Really! Did they really think that she would be more persuasive, that he wouldn't see through this ploy? What a picture it must have been—this pair of trusted followers hiding behind their mother, hoping to cut a deal for the best seats in the house. And finally, to top it off the other disciples heard about the stunt and were furious, perhaps because they were offended that the sons of Zebedee had been so bold as to use their mother to do their bidding, or perhaps because they regretted that these two birds had beat them to the punch, acting on something that they all were thinking about doing. I don't know, but it was certainly messy, and Jesus must have been shaking his head in disbelief.

So, how did Jesus respond to this series of little stings? First, he engaged rather than dismissed them. He explained to James and John that they didn't really know what they were asking, even though they assured him that they did. And he told them that in an ultimate sense, it wasn't his decision to make, which was another way of saying that things work differently in his kingdom. Things are turned on their heads. And then he lovingly called all his disciples together and taught them. He didn't rebuke them; he taught them—yet again. In the face of self-promotion, guile, suspicion, and envy, he listened, explained, and taught about the upside-down kingdom, seeing more in his disciples than they saw in themselves. Rather than giving a reprimand or a rebuke, he turned the stings into a teaching moment, affirming both his mission and his relationship with them.

On the Cross

I hesitate to even bring up the crucifixion of Jesus in a chapter about little stings. Surely, being crucified is no small matter, and his selfless act is the greatest gift known to humanity, but there is an aspect of this story from Scripture that I do want to mention. As Jesus was being executed, slowly, painfully, the Roman guards were dividing up his clothing among themselves by casting lots (Luke 23:34). While Jesus was hanging there in agony, the soldiers were playing a game of sorts in plain view with his clothes as the prize, probably the only worldly possessions he had. He did travel lightly.

Clothes are personal, and there is a feeling of infringement or violation of personal space, a little sting, when someone uses your clothes without permission. I would see my college roommate walking across the quad wearing my shirt and jacket, items he had taken from my closet without permission, things that I had planned to wear later that day. It stung, and I didn't like it. I can't even imagine how it would feel to see strangers dividing up the only things you own. It was an intentional part of the process for the guard, designed to provide a few extra little stings to the one being tortured. It must have added insult to injury.

So, how did Jesus respond? With the soldiers in his gaze, he asked God to forgive them, noting that they didn't know what they were doing. What an act of kindness and grace. When we pray daily for God's help from minding or giving little stings, we are praying that God's love and grace would be evidenced in us and through us, returning kindness instead of retaliating in kind. In this regard, I think we, all of us, are a work in progress, and I truly believe that God is eager to walk with us on our spiritual journey. We don't have to go it alone.

Some Practical Advice

Before we conclude this chapter and consider some questions for reflection and discussion, I want to offer several words of practical advice. I've tried to make the case in this chapter that words matter, and they can leave a nasty sting. Teasing, jokes, and pranks can quickly get out of hand, and can be too easily accepted and dismissed as harmless when, in fact, such activities, even when cloaked in good-natured ribbing, have a dark side. My advice is to avoid them when at all possible, and look out for situations where others with less power and influence are being subjected to and marginalized and hurt by such behaviors. Sometimes you just have to step forward and say, "That's enough. This needs to stop—now." If your concern is recognized, it can often lead to opportunities for meaningful, healing conversations.

Another area where words matter is criticism—given and taken. Of course, criticism when used for correction, to improve performance or promote safety, is a good thing. We can all use constructive criticism, so learning to receive and benefit from it is important. However, criticism can also be a thinly disguised way to belittle and marginalize someone, and the impact is cumulative. If you encounter or observe this kind of criticism, it is important to address the behavior before it gets out of hand. Simply put, undue criticism kills the spirit. We cannot be a party to such behavior.

I've also noted in this chapter that silence has a language and impact all its own. It can be used to demean, isolate, even make someone invisible—little stings with huge repercussions. Yet, it is so easy to ignore or simply overlook such behavior, even when doing so leaves someone in a tough situation. Perhaps you are noting a theme in this section. The vital practical advice I want to leave with you is this: our words and actions matter, they cast a long shadow. For those of us who beseech God's help to neither mind or return little stings, it behooves us to be present and mindful as we go through our day. Too often, these little stings pass by under the radar, treated as having little consequence, so they don't receive the attention they deserve. But they do matter. Actions that marginalize, mistreat, or tear down have no constructive place in our world. Loving God with all our hearts and our neighbors as ourselves will require all of us to be vigilant in the little things in our daily lives, especially those that come with a stinger.

Conclusion

At the end of the day, praying for God to preserve us from minding little stings or giving them requires intentional work on our part, too. As it turns out, it is no small matter. We are all recipients of God's grace, and the challenge for all of us is to live in that grace and allow that grace to flow through us, even as it changes us and challenges us to love our neighbors as much as we love ourselves.

And if I were to put a name on something to accompany us on this graceful spiritual journey, it would be kindness. If each of us are intentional each day to ask God to help us to be kind, to practice kindness as a fundamental way of being in this world, I believe we will be on the road to loving our neighbors in the midst of little stings and bringing the honey that blunts the unkindness in others. I pray that it may be so, even while I recognize that it is not an easy thing we ask for. May we pursue it nonetheless.

Questions for Reflection and Discussion

1. Can you think of a time when you were stung by words? How has this played out for you? Is there any corrective action or forgiveness that needs to take place?

2. What would happen if we, all of us, went through the day looking for those who are on the margins—belittled, diminished, or excluded by little stings? What would happen if we made this hunt a daily habit? Could this be part of what it means to love our neighbors?

3. Can you think of a situation where silence is used as the tool of choice? Is it time for you to break the silence? If so, how?

4. How do you manage the little stings that come your way, knowing full well that they can't all be avoided? Does approaching your day with the intent to be kind help at all, or is this just naïve?

5. In the midst of the swarm, how do you keep from returning the stings? Do you have role models and mentors who provide guidance for you? If not, where might you look for them?

FOR TODAY

O God:
Give me strength to live another day;
Let me not turn coward before its difficulties or prove recreant to its duties;
Let me not lose faith in other people;
Keep me sweet and sound of heart in spite of ingratitude, treachery, and meanness;
Preserve me from minding little stings or giving them . . .

Part II

ON DOWN THE ROAD

We started this spiritual venture together by praying a simple, honest, and desperate prayer, "Oh God, give me strength for another day!" It is the prayer you pray when you are in the ditch, just trying to make it through the day and get home by dark. In part 1, we dealt with some of the difficulties that complicate our lives when we find ourselves stuck in the mud: losing courage before difficulties, proving recreant to duties, losing faith in other people, enduring ingratitude, treachery, and meanness, and minding and giving little stings. When we face tough times, these complications can keep us pinned down, not allowing us to get back on our feet and move on down the road. Hopefully, we have gained some insight, resolve, and courage to face these difficulties squarely and honestly, and we are mindful that it is not in our own strength that we take this journey. God is with us, Immanuel, bringing hope and healing to us and through us. We are never alone.

In part 2, we will look at some practices that will give us energy, support, and direction for the road ahead: keeping a clean heart, facing failure with honesty and courage, seeing good in all things, receiving a new vision, and regaining the spirit of joy and gladness. These are renewing spiritual practices that ultimately allow us to give back, too, to be the cup of strength to other suffering souls. After all, when someone is in the ditch and we see their difficulties and hear their story, we can honestly say, "Me, too. I've been there." Sometimes, that's all that needs to be said.

So, let's start the journey—out of the ditch and on down the road.

7

Keeping a Clean Heart

Blessed are the pure in heart, for they will see God.
—MATTHEW 5:8

Introduction

When I heard that some of the kids at school received an allowance, money their parents actually gave to them for no particular reason other than to do a few chores around the house, I could hardly believe it. It seemed too good to be true. I never received an allowance, and the idea of having some spending money of any kind was usually out of the question. Once in a while, my mother would give my brothers and me a quarter each to go to the municipal swimming pool if we hoed five rows of corn in the garden, but that was the extent of it. Honestly, we had a loving and supportive family life and there was always good food on the table and clean clothes in the closet, but there wasn't any extra money for extravagances like allowances. We lived paycheck to paycheck, and my parents fretted far more than I knew about running out of money before the end of the month. So, I decided to earn my own spending money. At the age of thirteen, I became an independent businessman—peddling papers for the *Saginaw News*.

As it turned out, it was a good opportunity to learn about the world of business. I stopped by the newsstand each afternoon and picked up the papers for delivery. Once a week, I would go around to my customers and collect what was owed, and then go back to the newsstand to pay my own bill. Anything left over after the bill was paid belonged to me, my pay. Of course, if you couldn't collect from a customer or two, it cut into your earnings. As I think back, it seems the young paperboys took all the risks. The newsstand got paid in full each week regardless of how much I was able to collect. So, I faithfully paid my bill of $34.25 to Mrs. Patterson each week, the proprietor of the newsstand, and while I could make as much as $10 each week (that was the big recruiting slogan), I rarely made more than $6, and usually less, because not everyone would pay up. I learned quickly that my success depended on my own ability to find my customers at home with some cash on hand. It wasn't as simple as my boss made it out to be. Still, it was honest work, and it taught me discipline, responsibility, initiative, and patience.

One week, I stopped by the newsstand to pay my bill. I had my cash separated into little pockets in my money pouch: $34.25 for Mrs. Patterson and the rest for me. I stood in line along with several other paperboys, but when I got to the front of the line, she looked at her ledger, smiled at me, and said, "Well, I see that you have already paid your bill for this week. See you next week." I knew that I hadn't paid my bill yet, but instead of protesting, I simply headed back home with some extra cash in my pouch. It was my lucky day, I thought. I hid the money in a drawer in my bedroom, and while I must have spent the money little by little on something, I honestly have no recollection of how the money was spent. I never told anyone what happened, but it would come to mind from time to time. I kept telling myself that it was just a small thing—her mistake, not mine.

Fifteen years later, I received a promotion and joined the management team at the bank where I worked. One of my new responsibilities was to manage the cash in the bank vault. During my orientation, the president of the bank looked me squarely in the eyes and told me that he thought I would be a good bank officer as long as I remembered that the money in the vault didn't belong to me. In his own words, "You'll do fine as long as you remember that it's not your money." As I drove home that evening, Mrs. Patterson came to mind once again. I took advantage of her mistake, and I made her money my own. I had to make it right.

The next time I went home to visit my parents, I stopped by Mrs. Patterson's house. She looked surprised when she answered the door, and said, "You're an Allen, aren't you? Patrick, I think?" "Yup," I replied as my words just tumbled out, "and Mrs. Patterson, I have a confession to make.

I owe you some money. You see, fifteen years ago, you thought I paid my paper route bill one week but I didn't—$34.25, so here's a $50 bill. I'm so sorry. Please forgive me."

"Well," Mrs. Patterson responded, "I appreciate the gesture, but I can't take your money because you don't own me anything—actually you owe your mother. You see, I stopped by your house after my cash deposit was short exactly the amount of your weekly bill. Your mother went into your room and came back saying that you had the money in your dresser drawer. She wrote me a check for the full amount and that was that. We never talked about the incident again."

Wow! I was stunned, embarrassed, and humbled. This restitution thing was going to be harder than I had imagined. I sheepishly went back home and waited for a chance to talk to mom alone. Later that evening as we were doing the dishes, I told mom that I stopped by Mrs. Patterson's house to settle an old account, but she said that the bill was already paid. Mom kept on washing the dishes and said, "Yes, I found the money and paid the bill with a check. I left the money where I found it, believing that you would do the right thing some day—and you have. I knew you would." As I blinked the tears from my eyes, I pulled out the $50 bill and laid it on the counter. "Oh," she said, "that's too much." "No," I insisted, "it's been fifteen years, so this only makes up for inflation." She took the money, put it in her apron pocket, and gave me a hug.

At church that Sunday, there was a special offering for the youth group. They needed support for a summer missions trip, a venture that would impact their Christian walk and mold their character. I saw my mother slip the $50 bill into the offering plate and pass it down the row. I quickly pulled out my wallet and put another $50 bill in the plate. Mother looked at me with that motherly look and shook her head as if to say, "No, that's not necessary." I grinned and whispered, "Consider it an interest payment on an old loan." She nodded and whispered, "Paid in full."

From time to time, I would see Mrs. Patterson when I came home for a visit, and when I did I gave her a smile and a hug. She would always say, "It's so good to see you back home." And, indeed, it was. Wiping the slate clean may come at a cost, but living with a clean heart is priceless.

* * *

In this chapter, we will examine what it means to keep a clean heart, to be pure in heart as the Sermon on the Mount puts it (Matt 5–7). There are some predictable patterns that get us in trouble, and thankfully there are some simple but courageous things we can do to move beyond the cycle of failure, guilt, and shame that burdens us and slows us down. To pray for God's help in keeping a clean heart is certainly a bold and confident expression of faith in a God who wants us to live abundantly. Of course, some of this work is humbling but the promise is that the pure in heart shall see God—at work in our own lives, in the lives of others, and in our churches and neighborhoods, too. This is my prayer for all of us, that we shall see God. Let's begin.

Help Me to Keep My Heart Clean

When we pray, asking God to help us keep our hearts clean, what exactly do we want God to do for us and in us? What is a clean heart in the first place, and how do we keep it so, if that is at all possible? I confess that I've come to believe that it is more than possible. In fact, it is God's intention for us—to be holy, but it takes a real commitment of time and intention—and God's loving care and help, too. We'll begin by looking at the word—*heart*—and as we shall see, it is as central and vital to our spiritual well-being as the organ that pumps life-giving blood is to our physical well-being. Then, we'll turn our attention to the meaning of a "clean heart" and some spiritual practices to keep away from a daily cycle of failure and frustration that keeps many of us far too often and far too long in the ditches of life.

Having Heart

The Greek word for heart, *kardia*, refers to both the physical heart and the spiritual center of life. I've come to understand that the two are connected more than we even know. In fact, all of life is connected in deeply spiritual ways. Certainly, when the physical heart is functioning properly, it aids in clarity of thought and actions, words and deeds; and when it isn't, much of our passion and good intentions can be quickly derailed. In Scripture, we find some form of the word *kardia* used over eight hundred times, referring to certain aspects of the spiritual center of life.

Clearly, even when referring to our own inner life, heart can be used in so many different ways that its meaning is difficult to pin down. For example, we can speak of having a broken heart, a hard heart, a wicked heart, or even having no heart at all. We can plead with someone to have a heart, meaning to extend some kindness or compassion, to give someone a break. We can say that we carry someone in our heart, as a tender or precious memory. We can refer to someone as "my heart," indicating a deep and profound love or connection. We can describe someone as having a good heart, meaning their intentions, actions, and character are pure, above reproach. We can encourage others to take heart. And we can say that someone has the heart of a champion or a heart for ministry, or that their heart just isn't in the task at hand, whatever that task might be.

So, having heart can refer to either internal conditions or external behaviors—or both, our intentions and motives, our desires and passions, our thoughts, our actions, our commitments, even our character, and they can be holy or wholly destructive. When we pray, asking God for help in keeping our hearts clean, we are asking for divine assistance to keep a healthy and grace-filled alignment between our internal conditions and our external behaviors, to act in consistently good and healthy ways. In essence, we are asking for help to become persons of integrity, holy persons. In my view, it is one thing to become a Christian, but another thing altogether to embody a deep sense of the holy in our lives, to be like Christ. Deep down, I believe we all want to be holy, to respond to that sacred calling for our lives, for we know that the pure in heart shall see God. And we do want to see God, not only at the end of our journey, but while we journey, too. If Immanuel, God is with us, means anything, it means hope, healing, and grace as we journey, even if we don't know where we are going, and that is most of us.

So, where do we start if we want to keep a clean heart? Let's take a look in the closet where all the things that you don't talk about are stored.

Having a Clean Heart

The Greek word *katharos* means to be pure or clean, unstained, blameless, not guilty. And it can be taken literally, ceremonially, or spiritually. That is to say, a person can take a bath and be literally clean; undergo a waiting period accompanied by sacrificial offerings, washings, or other sacred rituals and be pronounced ceremonially clean by some religious authority; or stand before God with a pure heart and be spiritually clean. It is in this latter sense that we are intending when we pray to God, "Help me to keep my heart clean."

Such a prayer, if it is to be taken seriously by God and by each of us, demands our honesty and humility. The Apostle Paul confesses, "I do not understand what I do. For what I want to do I do not do, but what I hate I do" (Rom 7:15). This is a poignant confession that we don't always do what we know to do, but sadly do just the opposite. We have all done that from time to time. And Proverbs asks rhetorically, "Who can say, 'I have kept my heart pure; I am clean and without sin'?" (Prov 20:9). The answer is clear—no one the writer knows, at least not of their own doing. And John adds this pronouncement to any of us who think we are perfect, "If we claim to be without sin, we deceive ourselves and the truth is not in us" (1 John 1:8). What is clear is that if we are bold enough to ask God to help us keep a clean heart while fully acknowledging our own frailties and limitations, it is, indeed, a bold prayer.

Thankfully, John does not conclude at this point, at a point of desperation and deeper-than-doom despair. He continues with a wonderful promise, "If we confess our sins, he is faithful and just and will forgive us our sins and purify us from all unrighteousness" (1 John 1:9). Now that's good news! There is a place, a graceful place, for humility and honesty, and God responds to us where we are, not where we would like to be. In the story of the prodigal son's homecoming, the father didn't demand that the son take a bath before he wrapped his arms around him and gave him a great hug. God will meet us on the journey home, too.

So, where does all of this leave us? Clearly, we cannot simply determine that we will produce a clean heart totally of our own accord. That's silly. We need grace and forgiveness and divine help, but a clean heart is something we can strive for, ask for, despite of and in full view of our human frailties and failings. David was full of remorse when he wrote, "Create in me a pure heart, O God, and renew a steadfast spirit in me" (Ps 51:10). This was just after he had been confronted about his actions that intentionally took an innocent man's life. We'll discuss this story in more detail in the Scripture portion of this chapter, so suffice it here to say that despite his failings, he asked God to renew his spirit and create in him a clean heart. There were consequences for his actions, of course, but as far as I know, God faithfully answered David's heartfelt plea. And we find this promise in Ezekiel, "I will give you a new heart and put a new spirit in you; I will remove from you your heart of stone and give you a heart of flesh" (Ezek 36:26). I think we should all claim this promise as our own, trusting God to remove our hearts of stone and give each of us a heart of flesh, alive, full of humility and gratitude and grace.

If we truly want a clean heart, we will have to deal with something that we don't like to even talk about—sin, our actions that put us in the downward cycle, starting with poor decisions and ending up with secrets stowed away in our spiritual closets. There, they simply take up space and sap our spiritual energy. Just like the Apostle Paul, we do what we do not want to do, that which we know we should not do. And when we do, there is usually deception involved. We involve ourselves in actions that we wouldn't want anyone to see. We say we were doing one thing when in fact we did something altogether different—in secret. We say that we were in one place when in fact we were somewhere else. We say that we were with someone when in fact we were with someone else. We say that we were given that money or those supplies when in fact we took them. We say that we were only trying to keep the boss informed when in fact we were undercutting and hurting another team member. I could go on and on, of course, but I think you get the point. We make poor decisions, intentional choices, and then cover them up with deceit and outright lies. The result is another secret that we don't want to talk about taking up residence in our spiritual closet. Sometimes, as in the case of my theft of Mrs. Patterson's newspaper money, a secret can stay in the closet for decades—even longer, but they don't go away. They stand as witnesses to our failures, poor choices, and downright sins, and they beg our attention. Surely, if we want a clean heart, we have to clean out the closet. And if we are bone honest, most of us have something we need to take to the dump.

In ancient times, purity was thought to be achieved by one of two processes—fire or pruning. For most of us, it is a fire (a crisis) that forces us to publicly and honestly face the secrets in our closets. After some time, the truth comes out about a lie we've been nursing or a secret we've been hiding. Sometimes we're caught in the act of cutting moral corners, and in the heat and pain of the fire we must face the music. Such a fire is humiliating and humbling, and the burns hurt. The pain is real, of course, and sadly it spreads to those around us, too. It can result in lost jobs, squandered opportunities, and damaged or severed relationships. Sometimes, something very good is permanently lost, and the pain of a broken relationship can continue to disrupt lives for generations. Our decisions do have a moral trajectory; sin takes us somewhere, and not to healthy places where we want to live or be found. There is no way or no need to sugarcoat this reality. We are accountable for our actions.

However, if faced with courage, the fire can bring healing, too. Things won't necessarily just go away or return to normal, but over time there can be a new normal. Despite the pain and suffering, and in some cases because of it, a new normal can be established—one with a clean heart. Memories and regrets will persist and revisit us from time to time, but the pain will gradually subside as we embrace the forgiveness and healing that God and others extend to us, and that we extend to ourselves, too. This is perhaps the most difficult thing to do.

Pruning seems to be a much better option than fire to me. Instead of hiding secrets in our closet and locking the door with the hope that no one will see what is inside, why not open the door and clean it out? Why not face up and squarely deal with those things we don't want to talk about or let anyone see? Of course, it can be painful, it probably will, but waiting for a fire to break out is not a helpful or hopeful option either. The time to deal with the items hidden in our spiritual closets is now, today. We prune roses in the winter with spring in mind. Pruning brings new growth. If we want to have a clean heart, we must first cut away the dead branches. The pruning process begins with recognition, then repentance (reorientation, turning in a new direction), and, if necessary, restitution. The result will be freeing—a restoration, a clean closet and a clean heart.

Keeping a Clean Heart

Having a clean heart is one thing; keeping a clean heart is quite another thing altogether. I get that. At times, one wonders if it is even possible to do so, and some Christian traditions have decided that it isn't. Instead, it is simply an endless cycle of sin and repentance, enacted weekly or even daily. It seems to me that God intends more for us and from us than just an endless repetitive cycle of failure and recovery; he calls us to be holy. The word "holy" is found in Scripture over 1200 times so it isn't just a throwaway or throw-in word, and the Apostle Peter is quite direct about God's intent, "But just as he who called you is holy, so be holy in all you do; for it is written: 'Be holy, because I am holy'" (1 Pet 1:15–16). Here, Peter is most likely referring to verses in Leviticus where the call to be holy is repeated on at least six different occasions.

Of course, this can be intimidating and discouraging. So, when we pray, asking God to help us keep our hearts clean, where do we start? I think the starting point is to be clear that purity of heart deals with intention, not perfection. We will never be perfect in all we do, but our intentions and motives can be pure. When we ask for God's help, we must rely on God's provision. God does not ask us to do the impossible, but rather challenges us to do more than we think we are able to do. We start with the recognition that it is a divine partnership, not a solo task.

But we do play a critical role—it is not all up to God either. We are admonished in Proverbs to guard our heart because everything flows from it (4:23), everything; and during the Sermon on the Mount, Jesus cautioned all of us to be mindful of where we store up our treasures because that is where our hearts will be, too (Matt 6:21). We need to pay attention daily, to be intentional about the call to be holy. To stop, look, and listen for that still small voice that will push and guide us to be a certain kind of person, mindful of what is true, noble, right, pure, lovely, admirable, excellent and praiseworthy (Phil 4:8–9). If we are to keep our hearts clean, our hearts and minds must be in sync, to have integrity or wholeness. It is a daily discipline, a journey, not just a happy face we put on for Sunday worship. It requires that we be honest about our failures and weaknesses, and to make amends when necessary, but to be tender and kind with others and ourselves, too. When we pray for God's help to keep our hearts clean, it is not a prayer prayed in vain. It is a prayer of intention, of conviction, and with eternal possibilities.

Seeing God

Before we look at several stories from Scripture that speak to all of us about keeping our hearts clean, I want to take a moment to point out what I have come to believe is one of the most encouraging promises Jesus made to us. Early in his public ministry, he went up on a mountainside, sat down, and began to teach anyone who would listen. This discourse, found in Matthew 5–7, is known as the Sermon on the Mount, the most powerful sermon I know. Jesus began with a set of promises (the Beatitudes) including the one serving as an epigraph for this chapter: "Blessed are the pure in heart, for they will see God" (Matt 5:8). What a promise! The pure in heart shall see God. When we pray, asking God to help us keep our hearts clean, we are asking to see God, too, and the promise is that we will.

But what does it mean to see God? Will we see him in a burning bush or a wind storm or a volcanic eruption? That would be remarkable, but probably not. God does not need to impress anyone, including us. Instead of looking for God in all his kingly majesty and power and authority, I have come to believe that we see him best when we are still, quiet, and intent on first hearing his voice, even if from a distance. Waiting, watching, and listening are practices that bring us closer to God, and more able to recognize his voice and respond to his promptings.

If we wait and watch carefully and prayerfully, see God we will, in the faces of those we encounter each day, in our neighborhoods, in our work, in our churches, and in the good and not-so-good days that come our way, glimpsing God being God, active and gracious, bringing hope and healing to a desperate world. We will see God at work when the truth is told, when grief is expressed, and when hope is professed in a world where pretense, denial, and despair are the order of the day. As we pray to keep our own hearts clean, God is at work in us and through us. When we are intentional about this spiritual journey, God will meet us on the road, wherever that road takes us. And when we get there, wherever there is, the good news is that God is already there and at work.

Ultimately, we need not be satisfied with seeing God at a distance, catching a glimpse of his work here and there while peaking around a rock or hiding our faces in our hands as he passes by. No, we are called to be holy, and we want to be close to God, seeing him face to face as a friend sees a friend. The good news is that this is indeed possible but it takes intention, humility, resolve, and, above all, time. In my view, the call to holiness, to be a holy person, is a lifetime journey. It doesn't just happen, and for most of us, including me, it doesn't happen overnight, but happen it can and will. The promise is that the pure in heart will see God, and I am convinced that Jesus didn't have in mind some type of drive-by with a wave-and-a-smile encounter. No, if the incarnation means anything to us, it means that God became flesh and lived among us with grace and truth (John 1:14), wanting to see each of us face to face. The quest begins for each of us with the desire for a clean heart, and a daily request for God's help to keep it that way.

Scripture

Before we turn our attention to some words of practical advice and some questions for reflection and discussion, I want us to look at three short stories from Scripture that examine and illuminate different lessons to be learned about keeping a clean heart—and in doing so, seeing God. We will look first at the story of King David and Nathan, then the story of a woman caught in adultery, and finally a quick look at some of Job's trials and tribulations. As you will see, each story has something important to teach us.

David and Nathan

Nathan was a prophet in David's court. Generally speaking, he was there to provide both support and accountability for the king, bringing messages from God. At times, he brought messages of encouragement and guidance, and at other times he spoke words of caution and rebuke. As you might imagine, these latter words, even though they were from God, were brought with a certain amount of trepidation since it was never clear how the king would react. The prophet had a message from God, but the king had all the power.

In 2 Samuel 11–12, we find the story of David and Bathsheba, not one of the king's prouder moments. King David saw Bathsheba bathing on an adjacent rooftop and decided he must have her, despite the fact that she was married to someone else. Not long thereafter, the report came to him that she was pregnant. At first, David tried to trick her husband into thinking that the baby was his, but when that didn't work he gave orders to have the husband stationed at the very heart of the battle, thus insuring his demise. Then, Bathsheba moved into the palace.

Of course, this did not sit well with God, so Nathan the prophet came to David and told him a story about a rich man who had a large flock of sheep but took a poor man's only lamb to feed a visitor, a lamb that was like a member of his family. David was livid and swore that the man should make restitution before he was put to death. Nathan looked him straight in the eyes and told the king that the story was actually about him, the man who took another man's wife. What a powerful confrontation!

At this point, David has several options open to him. After all, he was the king. He could have killed the messenger, but he didn't. He could have dismissed Nathan and ignored the message, treating Nathan as someone who was not to be trusted as reliable, but he didn't do that either. Instead, the powerful king simply bowed his head and contritely said, "I have sinned against the Lord" (2 Sam 12:13). Nathan told David that God would forgive his transgression, but there would be a price to be paid. His son would not live—and he didn't. Surely, David remembered this tragedy the rest of his life, even to his grave.

An interesting side note to this story occurs years later. When David was close to death, he needed someone he could trust with his kingdom to take and anoint Solomon as the next king. Guess who David chose? You're right—Nathan. Truth tellers are not always popular, but they are trustworthy.

I don't think I need to connect all the dots here, so suffice it to say that when we are confronted with our own unclean behavior, we have a choice to make, too. We can kill the messenger by attacking the character of the person or the credibility of the message. We can simply deny and dismiss the message as irrelevant and misguided, or we can contritely admit our actions and accept the consequences they bring, being purified by fire. Very likely, there will be some difficult days, but a clean heart can be restored.

A Woman Caught in Adultery

The story of the woman caught in adultery is found in John 8:1–11. The earliest manuscripts and many other ancient witnesses do not mention this story, but I have included it here anyway, not to argue whether or not it should be taken literally (I honestly do not know if it actually happened), but because the story makes a point that I want us to take seriously. Certainly, this story has been taken seriously since at least the fourth century. That's good enough for me.

You may recall the story. A woman caught in adultery is brought to Jesus by some teachers of the law and the Pharisees. It is a crowded scene. They report that the Law of Moses commands them to stone her, and asks Jesus what they should do. Of course, it was a trick question, designed to trap Jesus. He bends down and writes something in the dirt, and tells them to go ahead but the one without sin should throw the first stone. One by one they leave the scene, the older ones first. With no one left to condemn her, Jesus sends her on her way, admonishing her to leave her life of sin.

What a remarkable story. There are many points that could be made, but I want to point out only one. Jesus didn't congratulate the men for zealously keeping the law, serving as public watchdogs by bringing the woman before the crowd to face accusations, humiliation, even death. Instead, he confronted the accusers about their own unclean hearts. It is not surprising to me that the older men, faced with Jesus' searching words, left the scene first. Hopefully, age brings some humility and insight. When we ask God to help us keep a clean heart, it is a deeply personal matter, and it takes our full attention. We are not called to be the sin police for the entire community. God will be the judge; we're called to be the lovers.

Job

I have always been fascinated by the story of Job, found in the Old Testament book by the same name. If you are unfamiliar with this story, I do commend it to you. There is much there to chew on. For now, however, I want to focus our attention on just one facet of the story. According to the story, Job was a good man, blameless and upright—a man without guile or sin. He kept a clean heart, but he was beset with a number of terrible tragedies and disasters. He lost everything: his house, his cattle, his friends, his reputation, even his family. There's no other way to describe it other than to say that it was awful, simply awful.

So, why? Why did a good person like Job suffer such awful circumstances? Honestly, the book is not entirely clear at this point and this question has been debated by theologians for centuries, so I will not try to end the debate now. I doubt that I could even if I tried. What is clear, however, is that it was not because of any sin on Job's part. He kept his heart clear and suffered a series of simply terrible events anyway.

What can we take from this? I think it is vitally important to be reminded that keeping a clean heart is not an insurance policy from bad things coming our way. Christians are still part of the human race, and bad things will happen to all of us at one time or another. Life is messy. What is clear is that bad things are not a punishment from an angry God for things known and unknown, remembered and forgotten, so encountering tough times is not a barometer of our spiritual condition. Don't let others pin that one on you.

* * *

What can we say about these stories from Scripture? First, when we are confronted by our own failures and downright sin, we have a choice as to how we will respond. The temptation, of course, is to vent and blame the messenger. At the end of the day, however, the redemptive course of action is to face up to our own behavior honestly and humbly, whatever the consequences for doing so may be. Second, keeping a clean heart is a personal challenge for all of us. We need not and should not appoint ourselves to be the community or church constable, assigned to watch for the missteps of others. We are called to be the lovers; God will be the judge. And finally, facing difficult times is not a reflection of our spiritual condition, although tough times can sometimes be the result of our own doing. Don't let others convince you that you have an unclean heart just because life happens. Honestly, life is messy and happens to all of us from time to time. Our call is to be faithful, not perfect.

Some Practical Advice

Although there have been some words of practical advice salted throughout this chapter, I do want to call specific attention to five practical things you can do when and while you pray for God's help to keep your heart clean. The first is to be sure that your heart is clean. In other words, examine your closet to see if there is anything there that has been stored away, begging to be addressed. If there is, take it out and haul it to the dump. As painful as it may be, this is where we must begin. I carried my theft of Mrs. Patterson's money for years, but it did not go away, would not go away. In the end, I'm glad it didn't. So, I ask, what is in your closet?

If we are truly after a clean heart, it is much better to prune away the dead wood than face a raging fire. Don't wait for the fire. Far too often, the fire will rage out of control, damaging far too many relationships and opportunities. Better to prune and prepare for new growth. That is, replace the deadwood with disciplines, habits, and practices that build your spirit and fill your cup.

Keeping a clean heart is a team sport, not a solo event. Of course, it takes humility and trust to share your struggles with someone, but keeping it all inside isn't a prescription for success either. Find a spiritual director, counselor, or trusted friend in whom you can confide and who will hold you accountable. Look for mentors and models. No need to go it alone. In my view, if I'm going to climb a mountain, I want someone with me who has been to the top and knows the way up and back to base camp. Trusted relationships are a gift from God. We all need them.

Remember, there's a big difference between keeping our hearts clean and being perfect, a standard that no one can achieve and maintain. Don't be too hard on yourself or on others. If you slip up, correct the situation immediately, and remember that you are not called to be the moral police for your neighborhood or church. We're called to be the lovers; God will do the judging.

Look for God in all the usual places, and unexpected places, too. The promise is that the pure in heart shall see God. Believe it. Claim it. Count on it. Act on it. As we work to keep our hearts clean, we will see God being God—in our own lives, in the faces of others, and in our churches and communities. Take this promise and go on a daily God hunt. You won't be disappointed, I promise.

Conclusion

In this chapter, we've examined what it means to ask God to help us keep our hearts clean. As it turns out, if we are to have a clean heart we must clean out our spiritual closets, getting rid of those things that weigh us down and burden our spiritual journeys, even if no one else knows about them. As we emerge from difficult and even terrible times, we're happy to be out of the ditch and ready to head on down the road, but the reality is that most of us have some spiritual cleaning to do before we plan another trip. It's not realistic to work at keeping our hearts clean until we have a clean heart in the first place, and that takes some intentional work. And to be honest, there may be a price to pay along the way, but a clean heart is priceless.

At the end of the day, we rest on the promise that the pure in heart will see God, and we all want to see God—at work in our lives and in the lives of those around us, and in our neighborhoods and churches, too. The promise is that if we seek him, he will be found. Amen.

Questions for Reflection and Discussion

1. Most of us have some spiritual pruning or some closet cleaning to do. Do you? If so, what would be a good first step?

2. Do you have a mentor, role model, or Sherpa whom you trust to help you make the clean heart journey, and to help you stay on track? If not, where might one be found, knowing that it is not good to make this journey alone?

3. What could you do to bookend your day, starting each day with the conscious intention to keep a clean heart and ending each day with an honest evaluation and a grateful heart? Talk to a spiritual director or a trusted friend about how to get started if you are at a loss.

4. Why is it so easy for us to see the speck in the eye of someone else and so difficult to see the log in our own? How do we avoid becoming the spiritual police for our friends and neighbors instead of being the lovers and encouragers?

5. What if you embraced the promise that the pure in heart will see God, and then went on a heart-inspired God hunt for the next fifteen days? How could you set up reminders and markers for the hunt, and what do you think might happen? Are you willing to give it a try?

FOR TODAY

O God:
Give me strength to live another day;
Let me not turn coward before its difficulties or prove recreant to its duties;
Let me not lose faith in other people;
Keep me sweet and sound of heart in spite of ingratitude, treachery, and meanness;
Preserve me from minding little stings or giving them;
Help me to keep my heart clean . . .

8

Facing Failure with Honesty and Courage

> Success is not final, failure is not fatal:
> it is the courage to continue that counts.
> —WINSTON CHURCHILL

Introduction

In this chapter, we will examine what it means to face failure, a very public failure, the kind of failure that everyone knows and talks about. It is not something that any of us would wish to experience, but experience it we must from time to time. No one is immune from failure—no one. If it doesn't happen to you, it will happen to someone you know and love very much, and it will rock your world. Despite our very best wishes and efforts to the contrary, failures of this sort cannot always be avoided. Sadly, it is part of life.

In chapter 2, we discussed how courage can easily be lost when we face difficulties of any sort, and in the last chapter, we considered what it means to have and keep a clean heart regardless of what is in your spiritual closet, but what does keeping a clean heart have to do with an outward failure like losing your job, your marriage, your home, or a dear friendship, or going bankrupt, or having to close a church? As it turns out—everything. It is no coincidence that Phillips Brooks, the great Episcopal preacher who wrote "For Today" over one hundred fifty years ago, entwined the two this way: *Help me to keep my heart clean, and to live so honestly and fearlessly that no outward failure can dishearten me or take away the joy of conscious integrity.* This is an earnest prayer, and together we will look at some of the human dynamics that accompany outward failure, and how we can deal with them in such a way that the joy of conscious integrity is not only abundant but sustaining and life-giving, too. As we will see, a clean heart and the joy of conscious integrity are intimately related, literally two sides of the same coin. Before we begin this examination, however, I want to share my own story of outward failure.

The Broken Cake Plate Dome

When I joined my current university as provost, a fancy title for an academic dean or the chief academic officer, I felt that I was at the top of my game. You see, I had served in this capacity at several other institutions over the previous twenty years, and as far as I knew (and know) I had a strong record of developing, inspiring, and leading the faculty with a focus on quality, community, and faithful service. I loved my work and felt a deep call or summons to it, but soon after I arrived on campus, things began to fall apart. While my former relationships with university presidents were that of a close friend, colleague, and partner, it became evident early on that this would not be the case. I was a direct report, nothing more—not a partner, not a friend. And as it turned out, I was an irritating one at that. It seemed that I couldn't do anything right, and it was difficult to understand what was expected of me or how my boss wanted me to report and relate to him. It must have been difficult for him, too.

When the time came to renew my three-year contract, I was given a two-year contract instead and was told that all senior staff members were receiving two-year contracts until their strategic plan was submitted. Soon thereafter I found out that the other members of the senior team actually received three-year contracts, and my contract was not changed even after I submitted my strategic plan several times. Needless to say, that was a message, and I read it loud and clear.

In the final year of the two-year contract, my boss told me in no uncertain terms that he did not have the confidence in me that he had in the other members of the senior management team, and my next contract would be for one year only. Knowing that the senior team had already seen more than its fair share of turnover, it was clear to me that

I was on the hot seat, and it didn't take a mathematician to project that if your contract goes from three years to two years to one year, the next one would be zero. That is to say, I'd be out of a job. About the same time, I learned that several of my trusted direct reports were working behind my back and over my head with other senior officials, making decisions without my knowledge or input, important decisions that were mine to make. I struggled to make it through each day, praying "For Today" at the start of each day and often several more times before I made it back home—tired, stressed out, my cup empty. Deep down I knew it was time to make a change.

In one respect, the easiest thing to do would have been to go and find another job and move on. I did have a solid career track record and many good friends and contacts in higher education, so a change was certainly possible. In fact, I filled out some applications and received several good offers, but in the end I was reluctant to accept them. Honestly, I didn't want to move and start over again, and my wife was in the middle of a very fine seminary program, a program that I dearly wanted her to be able to finish. Moving on would make that possibility very difficult. The best option, it seemed to me, was to try to negotiate a transition to some other position in the university if at all possible and finish my career there. I proposed to my boss that I move into a faculty position, and I am truly thankful that he accepted my proposal. Still, it was a public failure of sorts. I left my senior position, having not accomplished what I had set out to do. In my view, it was an embarrassing failure in full view of the entire university community, and I was deeply wounded.

As you might expect, my arrival in my new department was met with a mixture of uncertainly, fear, suspicion, and concern. I didn't blame anyone. They had very little to say about the former provost joining them, and they didn't know if I was a mole, an informant, or just a discarded administrator. Still, they welcomed me, even if cautiously, and I began to prepare to teach—something I hadn't done full time in over twenty-five years. And much of the teaching was online. As you might expect, there was a steep learning curve for the former provost.

I knew that I would have to adjust to my new assignment, and I embraced it as a unique learning opportunity. What I didn't expect, however, is that I would become virtually invisible in a matter of minutes. After all, my former position was a prominent, powerful, and important one (at least in my own view), and I was "in the know" about almost everything. There was a certain status to being a senior administrator, but now I was in exile. My email messages dropped from about five hundred each day to less than ten, and the dozens of persons I counted as good friends turned out to be less than five. There were no waiting lines to get in to see me. In fact, no one came at all. Honestly, I was embarrassed and disappointed to step down from my position, a career-ending thud in full view of the campus community, but losing my identity was harder still. When someone asked me what I did at the university, I would tell them, "I teach in the doctoral leadership program in the School of Education," but then quickly add, "but I was the provost," as if that would somehow grant me a bit more status and credibility. Looking back, my response was very sad, but at the time I was earnestly praying, "Oh, God, give me strength to live another day." Clearly, I was in survival mode, trying to fake my way through in spite of my pain, embarrassment, and deep sadness.

Each summer, our program begins with a new cohort of doctoral students for a face-to-face summer intensive lasting several weeks. I was assigned to be the co-instructor for our newest cohort, teaching a leadership course. The department chair told me that with my experience in higher education, I would have much to offer our students. Of course, given the developments over the past several years, I felt like more of a failure than a leader. I really doubted that I had anything to offer. Still, I showed up on Monday with a smile and did my best to be cordial and positive. It took most of my energy to do so. The co-instructor told me that she had to be gone on Friday, so the class would be mine. I said, "Great!" but I was really feeling that I have very little to offer.

I worked all week to prepare for Friday, and the morning class (3 hours) went by quickly. I had twice as much material than I could possibly cover. The students were intent and appreciative as I offered them some important things to think about and to use in their own work settings. I must admit that I was feeling really good about the class and about myself when I packed up to leave—I was going to be alright. That morning, my wife baked a Bundt cake for the class, which of course was met with much gratitude and genuine enthusiasm. I brought the cake in a cake carrier, the kind with a glass cake dome that sits on top of a cake stand, but this version didn't have any grooves to hold the cake dome in place. On the way to the school, the dome was taped in place, but I forgot to secure the dome before I left after class. You can probably imagine what happened next. In the crowed hallway, right outside the lunch room where forty or so students and faculty were gathered, the glass cake plate dome slowly slid off the stand, hit the floor with a big crash, and shattered into a million pieces—scattering down the hallway. Of course, I was embarrassed, even though several students and staff members quickly jumped in to help me clean up the mess, but I felt something much deeper, something begging to be acknowledged. It hit me as I stood there surveying the broken mess, it was not just a cake plate dome that was on the floor smashed into pieces, my career, my identity, and my spirit were smashed into a million pieces, too. I had no idea how to clean up that mess.

I did not have much of an appetite, so I took a short walk before returning for the afternoon class. I could not have been away more than forty-five minutes, but when I opened my office door, there it was on my desk. A big white box with a note on top that simply read: From your Friends in the 2013 Cohort. Inside was a brand new glass cake plate dome. I just stood there with tears running down my cheeks—what a moment of healing and grace. A student told me later that they didn't want me to go home with a broken cake plate dome. And as it turns out, I went home with something else, too. I had a new identity, a new career, and a spirit that was starting to mend. Now, when I am asked what I do, I proudly say, "I'm a professor in our EdD program in leadership, and I just love to teach—and even more, I love my students. They are life-giving!"

* * *

This was a turning point in my own journey to get out of the ditch and on down the road. It didn't happen all at once, but that was the point where I started to focus on the road rather than wallowing in the ditch. In what follows, we will look at what failure means in our society, and the implications for us when we ask God to help us to live so that no outward failure can dishearten us or take away the joy of conscious integrity. As I will argue, we can't do so without a new mind-set and a clean heart. Ultimately, it starts with a right relationship with God.

Failure

We speak of many different kinds of failure. There is a failure of vision, a failure of nerve, and a failure of character. There's the failure to forgive, the failure to dream, the failure to believe in self or others, the failure to be dependable, and the failure to try something big—beyond our own expectations and comfort zone. And there are embarrassing public failures, too: a public reprimand or a demotion at work, a failed marriage, a loss of job or business or church, an expulsion from school, or a dismal speech or presentation. What they all have in common is that failure is something we try to avoid at all costs. We don't want to talk about our failures, although others' failures are certainly fair game to whisper about, and we don't want to be labeled a failure, a label that comes with so much personal and public baggage.

Many of us have been told by a parent or coach, "There is only one thing worse than a quitter—someone who won't try at all." What goes unsaid, however, is that failure is even worse. Not trying and quitting may be very poor decisions, but they are both so much better than failing, even if no one can explain why. Most of us grow up with a fear of failure that runs very deep. To fail is to be somehow diminished as a person, proving in some perverse way that we are less than we should or ever could be, a disappointment to ourselves and to others. Failure causes the voices in our heads to go off, bringing words of embarrassment, chastisement, and shame. It is certainly a wicked cocktail, resulting in a hangover of self-pity and humiliation.

Thus far, I haven't painted a very pretty picture of failure, the common portrait that is embedded deep in the inner recesses of our being, something to be feared. Yet, there is a different way to think about failure, a healthy and helpful reframing that takes failure out of the whispering shadows and into the light of day. Here, we can draw from the wisdom of entrepreneurs who have seen both successes and failures, many of them. What if we assumed that failures of some kind or another are inevitable, even common, much more common than we know because most failures are kept as private and secret as possible? What if we believed that failures have much to teach us, perhaps much more than our successes? What if we understood that we can embrace failure as a fact of life without being diminished as persons? What if in a culture where our successes are worshiped, we honored our failures, too? What if we openly and honestly talked about our failures and what we have learned from them—about God, about ourselves, and about our neighbors? What if we included our successes and our failures on our resumes, knowing that it is our failures that make us what and who we are today? Is it possible that we could think about failures in this way, or is it just a pipe dream?

Honestly, I think it is more than just possible, such an adjustment in our thinking is necessary, even required, if we are going to ask God to help us live so honestly and fearlessly that no outward failure can dishearten us or take away the joy of conscious integrity. When we pray such an intentional prayer, we are asking God to help us reframe our understanding of failure, to think about failure in a different way. We are asking for a new mind-set, one that understands failure to be a great teacher, a chance to encounter and learn and grow. A mind-set that recognizes that our future successes depend upon what we learn from our failures; that failure is never permanent; that failure can lead to humility, adaptability, and resilience. Failure can change us for the better. I call this mind-set *an extravagant embrace of failure*. If we take this mind-set as our own, we embrace our failures along with our successes with honesty and courage, and we don't live in constant fear of what others will think of us if we fail. The fact is, most of our colleagues and friends don't think of us nearly as much as we think they do. And even when they do, an extravagant embrace of failure begins with the understanding that our identity comes from God who loves us unconditionally and makes wild promises to us about our future, and not from those who stand in the shadows and whisper our names. God is with us for the long haul, and that includes every failure we encounter, even those of our own doing.

In the next portion of this chapter, we will examine what it takes to embrace failure in such an extravagant fashion, and what it has to do with a sense of conscious integrity and a clean heart. As we will see, you can't have one without the other.

Honesty and Courage in Failure

It goes without saying that no one wants to fail at anything. Why would we? Yet an extravagant embrace of failure begins with the knowledge that failure is not fatal; life will go on, but it is up to us to face our situation squarely and summon the courage to continue. How do we do this? We start, I think, with the recognition that failure *will* change us, and it *can* change us for the better. That is to say, we can be shaped in positive ways through failure if we are intentional, if we learn from our mistakes. We can become more compassionate, understanding, generous, forgiving, and concerned about others when they fail, and we can become humble and kind, too. We start by accepting our failure—we embrace it. This is not to say that we celebrate the mess we're in, but we acknowledge that we are where we are and it is what it is, and we can't change that fact. However, we do have choices. It is what we do now that will shape us for good or ill. We can't turn back the clock, but we can move ahead one step at a time.

The first step is to be bone honest about the failure, carefully assessing and taking responsibility for our part in whatever has heretofore transpired. It is easier and more entertaining to deny any responsibility and blame others for all our troubles, but that is seldom, if ever, the case. The first courageous act is to take ownership of our actions and admit our missteps and mistakes.

The second step is to carefully consider what happened, reviewing the steps that lead us to this failure. Seldom does a failure happen all at once or by surprise. There is usually a trail of missteps and ignored warning signs. What were they? What could we have done differently? How should we proceed now? How can we proceed? Is there anything we need to go back and say or undo; any type of restitution or apology or request for forgiveness? Of course, these are difficult and humbling tasks that take courage, but they set the stage for a turnaround. It is a good practice to take some time each morning to reflect and take stock, asking God to show us any blind spots or specific actions that we should undertake.

As we are hoping and praying for a turnaround, it is also helpful to let go of factors that are beyond our control. For example, we can't control how others will react to our failures or dictate how our story will be told to others. We simply can't, so there is no use in worrying about it or trying to manage the message. People will say what they will say. And we can't control how our friends, even our close friends, will respond. However, we will find out who our friends really are, and the sobering fact is that the number is usually quite small, usually counted on one hand. Time spent with God in solitude is helpful here, too.

Finally, dealing honestly and fearlessly with our failures is more productive when done in the company of those who love us and stand with us in no uncertain terms. While the temptation is to hide out and close off, it is precisely then that we need the wise counsel and support of others. Usually we're not the first to walk whatever road we are on, so it is helpful to have others who can point the way to healing, help carry our load, point out dangers along the way, and hold us accountable to deal honestly and fearlessly with our situation. Many times, healing and grace come in the form of relationships.

Usually, there's a long road ahead of us, and as with many things in life, time is a great healer. You can't rush the restoration of relationships, self-image, spirit, or identity. The damage can come quickly, but the healing takes time. However, the good news is that at some point, in good time, we do arrive at a turning point. If you ask anyone who has recovered from failure, they will tell you about a specific point in time when they made an intentional decision to go about things differently, or they had an insight into their situation and self-defeating behaviors. Or perhaps they received a word of encouragement, or someone said or did something that hit home, even a very small or seemingly insignificant thing that began a turnaround. It was the turning point when recovery from failure began in earnest. As the story at the beginning of this chapter tells, the turning point for me when I was dealing with the end of my administrative career was a simple act of kindness by some students who replaced a broken glass cake plate dome, maybe a fifteen-dollar purchase. However, the emotional and spiritual significance was worth a million dollars to me. From that day on, my life had a different trajectory, out of the ditch and headed on down the road. We don't forget such moments of grace, and hopefully we can someday be an instrument of grace in the lives of others, too. As we will see, it starts with a clean heart.

The Joy of Conscience Integrity

My parents were both raised on a farm during the Great Depression, and they carried with them a deeply held conviction about the importance of personal integrity in everything you do. They admonished my brothers and me repeatedly to always tell the truth, to keep our promises, to pay our debts, to honor our commitments, and to be loyal to our friends. "Your word is your bond," they would say, "and there is nothing more valuable in life than a clean conscience and an upright character. Sometimes that's about all you may have, but it is enough. No one can take that from you." Of course, I think they were right. They knew that a clear conscience is priceless, and there is a joy that comes from conscience integrity that will keep you singing, even during tough and difficult times. There is no substitute for a clean heart.

It is no coincidence that in "For Today," the request for a clean heart and the joy of conscience integrity are included in the same phrase: *Help me to keep my heart clean, and to live so honestly and fearlessly that no outward failure can dishearten me or take away the joy of conscious integrity.* Conscience integrity requires a clean heart, so we begin by cleaning out our spiritual closets as we discussed in chapter 7. When we do, the joy of conscience integrity will come, and it is indeed a blessing.

One of the joys of conscience integrity is that we have peace of mind. We don't have to worry about being found out when the phone rings or someone comes to the office door asking uncomfortable questions, or when we are summoned to the boss's office. We don't have to worry that the masquerade we have been promoting will crumble and we will be exposed for who we really are. Conscience integrity brings a joy that allows us to keep our heads held high, even in difficult times of outright failure. It is surely a peace that passes understanding.

Another important aspect of conscience integrity is that it allows us to tell our story of outward failure with honesty and courage, and there is a certain a joy that comes with sharing the story of your own turning point and how you got out of the ditch and on down the road. And sometimes all you have to say is, "Me, too. I've been there. I'll walk with you. God is faithful." And who knows, those words of encouragement might just be an important part of another's turning point, whether you ever know it or not. Surely that brings us hope and courage and joy. Grace works that way.

Scripture

Before I offer some words of practical advice, let's look at another incident in the life of the Apostle Peter, certainly not one of his better moments. In many ways, it is a story about all of us, too, providing insight as we pray daily to live so honestly and fearlessly that no outward failure can dishearten us or take away the joy of conscience integrity.

Peter's Denial

Peter, a former fisherman, was full of fire and passion, and he wasn't afraid of hard work. He wasn't easily intimidated either, and was always ready to fight on a moment's notice or even die for the cause. He was the person that Jesus knew could stand at the epicenter of unbelief, petty jealousy, persecution, and fear, and be the rock upon which the church would be built and flourish. Peter was someone who asked important questions and had a glimpse into the nature of Jesus' ministry and a vision of the coming kingdom. He was convinced that Jesus was the Messiah, but just what kind of messiah Jesus was to be was not entirely clear to him, nor anyone else for that matter. Certainly, he saw no need for Jesus to die at the hands of either the Jewish religious leaders or the Romans, but he did promise to be there with him, wherever there was: "Even if I have to die with you, I will never disown you" (Matt 26:35). He promised to be Jesus' rock, and in many ways, he was, at least until his promise was put to the test.

What happened next is a familiar story to most of us. Jesus was arrested and brought before Caiaphas and the entire Sanhedrin. Peter, Matthew tell us, followed at a distance. While Jesus was questioned, ridiculed, and tormented, Peter sat in the outer courtyard. There, a servant girl asked Peter if he was a follower of Jesus. "I don't know what you're talking about," was his response (26:70). In many ways, this was a question asked in private. Peter could have answered truthfully and most likely that would have been the end of it, but he didn't. Instead, he denied the obvious—the first step down a dark path that leads to nowhere but the ditch.

Sometime later that evening, another servant girl noticed Peter and pointed him out to those standing there as a follower of Jesus. Now the stakes were higher; it was no longer a private conversation—others were involved. So, Peter escalated his response, "He denied it again, with an oath" (26:72). It seems the more public the questions are, the louder the truth must be denied—this time with an oath. And when he was confronted about his identity a third time, he called down curses on his accusers. It was an obvious case of attacking the messenger. If it happened today, he would have threatened to call his lawyer and sue. And with each denial, he responded with more intensity and self-righteous indignation, simply digging a deeper hole for himself. In the end, it was obvious to all that he did know Jesus, and it was equally obvious that he could not be taken at his word, in spite of his ugly and aggressive protestations to the contrary. Peter went away and wept, which was perhaps his first honest response to all that had transpired that evening.

After his crucifixion and resurrection, Jesus appeared to his followers from time to time, but as far as we know, he didn't speak directly to Peter or meet privately with him. Surely, Peter must have been heartsick, feeling a deep sense of shame and embarrassment for his public failure to stand with Jesus as he had promised he would do. Sometime later, some of the disciples were out fishing in the Sea of Galilee. After all, this is what they knew to do, and honestly, what else could they do after they had all abandoned Jesus on that fateful evening not so long ago? According to John's Gospel, they fished all night without success, but someone from the shore called out and told them to throw out their nets on the other side of the boat. Although obviously tired and heading for shore, they did as they were instructed, and soon their nets were so full that they couldn't even pull them into the boat. In all, they caught 153 large fish.

John shouted, "It is the Lord!" (John 21:7) and Peter jumped out of the boat and headed for shore. There, Jesus had a fire going and cooked some of their fish, feeding the disciples, even Peter. Then, Jesus and Peter went for a walk along the shore. Jesus forgave Peter, reinstated his mantel of leadership, and urged him to feed the sheep, Jesus' sheep. In other words, he asked him to continue the work of building the church. What a powerful scene of forgiveness, grace, and restoration, and the turning point, as it so often is, began with a simple meal. Truly, there is something deeply spiritual about breaking bread together. If we are to take anything from this story of Jesus and Peter, it would be this: when there is an outward failure and relationships are fractured, start with a meal. Gather around a table, share some food, and look each other right in the eyes. I can assure you that Jesus will be there, too, bringing hope, healing, and grace, even in the midst of the most difficult conversations.

When we pray, asking God to help us live so honestly and fearlessly that no outward failure can dishearten us, the turning point can begin with a simple cup of soup and some crusty bread offered in the name of Jesus. When you are in the ditch, please don't disregard an invitation to come and dine. And if you are on the road to recovery, please open your table, tell your own story to those in need of encouragement, forgiveness, and healing, and share the joy of conscious integrity to anyone who will listen.

Some Practical Advice

There have been bits of practical advice offered throughout this chapter, so here I will list five salient words of advice to serve as a summary for quick reference. First, it is so important to understand that perfection in a spiritual sense does not mean that we are perfect in every way and in everything we undertake, that we make no mistakes and think no selfish thoughts at one time or another. No one is perfect in that sense. After all, we are all human, and becoming a Christian does not remove us from the human race. When the Bible speaks of being perfect, it means becoming mature, fully developed, growing with sincere intent, completed in

Christ. It is in this sense that we are called to be perfect, and a failure along the way does not mean that we are imperfect, needing to go back to the very beginning of our spiritual journey and start over. Failure is part of life.

Second, failures are the best teachers we will ever have, much better than our successes. If we embrace our failures with honesty, humility, and courage, we can become different persons—better persons. Although the voices in our heads will go off and we may feel shame when we fail, it is important to remember that these are learned responses. It is possible to embrace our failures with a helpful mind-set that sees failures for what they are—some of the most formative experiences we will ever encounter as persons of faith.

Third, if a failure has put you in the ditch, give yourself some time to recover. It takes time to heal, so don't be in too big a hurry to put it all behind you. Impatience is not a friend. When I broke my arm as a child, I was so impatient to get the cast off. I was told to be patient, because even though it looked and felt like nothing was happening, something was happening. The bone was healing. In fact, it would ultimately be stronger than it was before the break, but if removed too early, I would suffer a setback. Healing from a failure takes time, too, and hopefully we'll emerge stronger and more sensitive to the needs of others as well.

Fourth, focus on what you can control and do right now, not on what others did or on things that are beyond your control. Brooding and blaming can come so easily, but they sap your spirit and distract you from looking at your own part in what happened and what needs to happen next. Keep the focus close to home.

Finally, it is important that we tell our stories of failure, especially in communities of faith where the emphasis is on "happy church" each Sunday morning. If we are to be authentic followers of Jesus, we must somehow find ways to make room for lament and failure in worship along with praise and adoration. Feeling like a failure in church is one of the most lonely and alienating experiences I know. Perhaps a small group, with an emphasis on sharing a simple meal together on a regular basis, might become a safe haven where our stories and the joy of conscience integrity can be shared, offering examples of what it means to live honestly and fearlessly amid the failures of life.

At the end of the day, others need to hear that our successes are not final and our failures are not fatal: it is the courage to continue that counts—to live so honestly and fearlessly that no outward failure can dishearten us or take away the joy of conscious integrity.

Conclusion

In part 1, we dealt primarily with the earnest prayer for God's help to get through another day when we find ourselves stuck in the ditch. In part 2, we have been looking at how with God's help we can get out of the ditch and on down the read. As chapter 7 reminded us, it all starts with a clean heart, and in this chapter, a hard chapter in many ways, we examined outward failures and how to deal with them in such an honest and courageous way that we do not lose heart or the joy of conscious integrity.

Failure, as it turns out, *will* definitely change us, and it *can* change us in good and formative ways. In fact, we learn and grow much more from our failures than we do from our successes, particularly when we embrace our failures as a part of life, never fun but certainly not fatal, despite feelings to the contrary in the moment. The key is to honestly face our failures for what they are, avoid blaming and brooding, and courageously make amends when necessary and changes where needed. None of these steps can be rushed; they all take time. However, at just the right time, in the grace of time, we will come to a turning point where we stop wallowing in self-pity, make our way out of the ditch, and start heading on down the road. Such turning points are simply grace in action, sometimes mediated by a thoughtful act or a kind word or a spiritual insight or a kick in the pants from someone who cares for us. Sometimes it takes more than one.

Whatever the impetus, we do remember those turnaround times, and they are certainly worth sharing with others who are struggling with failure, too, especially in our communities of faith where tough times are often disguised in the midst of public worship. Honestly, most of us are not very good at talking about our failures, although we all have a story or two to tell. At the end of the day, what we can share is that we all encounter failures of various kinds, but if faced with honesty and courage and God's grace, we become better persons—more sensitive to the plight of others and the stories they tell, more disposed to help a stranger left in the ditch by the side of the road, more perceptive to God's leading, and more willing to share our own stories and the joy of conscious integrity that comes from a clean heart. This is a story that needs, no begs, to be told—life is messy, but God is faithful.

Questions for Reflection and Discussion

1. How would you explain to someone what is meant by an extravagant embrace of failure? Do you agree that the mind-set we have about failures largely determines how we respond when they come our way?
2. What stories of failure do you have to tell? If you were to construct your own resume of failure (not an exciting title), what would you list as the key things you have learned and ways you have changed through these events in your life?
3. Are there things undone that you need to address—someone you need to talk to, even if it hurts?
4. Why is it so easy to focus on the failures of others, but so difficult to face our own?
5. What is the one key takeaway from this chapter that you are going to employ as a spiritual practice?

FOR TODAY

O God:
Give me strength to live another day;
Let me not turn coward before its difficulties or prove recreant to its duties;
Let me not lose faith in other people;
Keep me sweet and sound of heart, in spite of ingratitude, treachery, or meanness;
Preserve me from minding little stings or giving them;
Help me to keep my heart clean, and to live so honestly and fearlessly that no outward failure can dishearten me or take away the joy of conscious integrity . . .

9

Seeing Good in All Things

> The Lord gives sight to the blind . . .
>
> —PSALM 146:8

Introduction

Open wide the eyes of my soul that I may see good in all things. What a wonderful prayer for all of us, certainly a good way to start out each day, but what do we mean when we refer to the eyes of the soul and how do we open them to see good in all things—even terrible things? In this chapter and the next, we will set our sights on spiritual understanding and discernment, on having our eyes wide open to God's work in us and through us, and a new vision of truth to guide us as we journey down the road called life. It is certainly good to be out of the ditch, but a clear spiritual vision is necessary as we navigate the roads ahead. The old Quakers have a saying, "Way will open in front of you, and Way will close behind you." Let's pray that we will have the wisdom and divine guidance to see the Way and know the difference between an open and a closed door, and what to do when the door is simply unanswered. As with other spiritual practices, there is some work for each of us to do, too.

In this chapter, we will start by thinking together about gaining spiritual insight before we examine what it means to see good in all things, at different times and in different places, and even in our pain and suffering. Before we do, however, I want to share a story that illustrates how the disappointments and disillusionments of the moment can shape us and result in personal growth, as unpleasant and unwanted as such events are to experience at the time. In fact, sometimes we have to look back to see God's fingerprints all over our lives, preparing us for a future that we cannot see.

Time to Go

I remember the worship service like it was yesterday. My wife and I had been praying for over a year for God's direction, to either give us new wind in our sails for the jobs we held or lead us to a new place of service. Deep down, we were a bit tired and restless, and I felt that I had done what I came to the university to do, so a move was certainly a real possibility. Still, we really did not know if that meant a local job change or a major move, and if so, when or where we might go.

While sitting in a chapel service at the university, I clearly heard God say to me, "You can go." I was stunned. Honestly, I am always a little suspicious when I hear someone say that God spoke to them, and it hasn't happened to me more than a time or two, but clearly, I heard a voice telling me to get ready for a journey. I found my wife after the service, and with tears in my eyes I told her that we had been released from our work at the university. We would be moving on. Where or when we would go, I had no idea, but I knew our days in San Diego were numbered.

When I returned to my office that morning, I had three telephone messages waiting for me, all from persons working to fill vacant presidential positions at Christian colleges. "Wow!" I thought to myself, "God isn't wasting any time!" I picked up the phone and called the first number. Bill, a consultant for a presidential search for a college in the South, answered the phone. He said that my name was at the top of their candidate list, and after doing some initial checking, he wanted to come to San Diego and spend the day with my wife and me. We met and really hit it off. So much so, in fact, that Bill asked us to clear our schedules later that same week to fly to the school and meet with the trustees. He felt that we were a perfect fit for the job. It was almost a done deal.

As we quickly made some flight reservations, however, I felt a bit uneasy about the pace of the interview process. So, when I called Bill, in addition to giving him the flight information, I said, "Bill, you didn't ask me, but I want to be sure that you know that I have been married before. I hope that isn't a deal-breaker." Silence, absolute stone silence on the other end of the line. "Hello," I said jokingly, and then I heard Bill give a big sigh and say, "Well, it is a big deal. After all, you're damaged goods. Nobody will want you." He hung up the phone without even saying goodbye. His words stung deeply and haunted me at night for quite a while—damaged goods. I had never thought of myself in those terms.

So much for message number one, but there were still two more to pursue.

The second message was from a retiring college president in the Midwest who was leading the search for his own replacement, ordinarily a red flag of sorts. But since I knew the institution and several of the faculty and senior administrators personally, I decided to return his call. Before I did, however, I took a look at the college website and was taken by all their new construction, including the impressive president's home on campus. I have to admit that I began to envision myself conducting fancy receptions in the president's home, particularly on my own inauguration weekend. Now I know that I was way down the road and way out of line, but there it is. The job seemed like a perfect fit for my commitments and skills, and I thought I could have a good run as the president there.

Early in the phone interview, I made sure to ask if they had any qualms about hiring a divorced person as their next president. "Of course not," was the answer. "We know you, Patrick, so there is no problem. All you have to do is come to a closed-door session of the board of trustees and share with them all the intimate details of your divorce, including any infidelity and other inappropriate acts on the part of your former spouse. We'll certify to the community that you are acceptable, and that will be that. How does that sound?"

Honestly, it didn't sound very good at all. Divorce for any reason is painful, and long ago I vowed that I would never say anything negative to anyone about that time in my life, even if it was to get a really good job with a really big house on campus. I politely said that such a meeting was out of the question, thanked the president for his interest in me, and bowed out of the search. The next day, he called me back and asked if it would be better if I just told him the unpleasant facts and he would certify to the board that I was ok. Again, I declined his offer. The more I thought about it, I really didn't think it would be a good fit for me to lead an institution that went about the business of certifying anyone.

So much for message number two.

With the first two possibilities out of the question, I turned my attention to message three. A prominent retired president was assisting a sister college with their presidential search, and my name was at the top of his list, too. (I began to wonder if they had all attended some type of presidential recruiters meeting where names of potential candidates were shared.) In any case, I was invited to interview on campus as one of two finalists. That was nice. What was not so nice, however, was that the school was small and struggling, firmly aligned with a different denomination and theological tradition than my own, and located in Alberta, Canada—a world away from my current assignment in San Diego in several respects. Still, remembering the word I received from God in chapel and with only one option remaining, I agreed to come for an interview.

Three days later, I was on the campus in Edmonton, working as hard as I could to put my best foot forward despite my sincere reservations. However, the longer I was with the search committee, the more it became obvious to me that I was not the right person for the job. They needed someone from their own tradition who could wholeheartedly embrace and articulate the theology and mission of the college to all its constituencies, inside and out. That I could not do. And given the backbreaking schedule, the difficulties, and the stresses that comes with any college presidency, I wanted my spouse to be excited and supportive of the move, too. But clearly, Edmonton was not on her destination bucket list. I shared my reservations with the chair of the search committee as we drove to the airport. She agreed. Now, it seemed, I was out of options altogether.

As I changed planes in Seattle on the return trip, I received a call from a fellow academic dean, a friend and colleague for years. In many ways, I served as a mentor to him, offering advice on how to approach a difficult situation or work with the president or dismiss a troubled faculty member. I told him that I was just getting ready to board the plane so I didn't have very much time to chat. "Oh," he said, "that's fine. I just wanted you to know that I just accepted the offer to be the next president of a very fine Christian university in the Midwest." As it turned out, it was the one with a big new president's home on campus—my message number two. "Well, congratulations!" I said with all the enthusiasm I could muster. "I know you'll be a great president. Way to go!" And I meant what I said. I was truly happy for him.

However, I boarded the plane a bit stunned. During the flight home I had time to sit in the dark, look out the window, and reflect on the events of the past several weeks. My initial thoughts were not so magnanimous—now my friend and colleague, my mentee, would be living and having receptions in my presidential home! It was just a short foray into self-pity. Before too long, I began to ask some serious questions. Did I really hear God speaking to me in that chapel service or did I just make it up? Did I simply hear what I wanted to hear? And what about the three messages on the same day? If that was God's leading, why did I end up with disappointment after disappointment, first being told in no uncertain terms that I was damaged goods, then made to feel like a misfit, then a poor fit, and then an outsider. What was all that about?

To be honest, to this day I still think about that three-message day, and I doubt that I will ever figure out why it all turned out the way it did, but was there good in this experience, too? Is it possible to see good in such things? Sometimes it takes time, but my answer is a resounding yes! I certainly learned many good things from the experience. I learned that it is important to take your time, even when you feel God's direct leading. I learned that everything will not always go as planned. Just because you have several opportunities before you, it is possible that none of them will pan out, and there may be other opportunities coming your way that you do not yet see. Look before you leap. That's good to remember.

I learned that I had a very high opinion of myself, and I could come across to others as having a big ego, even arrogant at times, and sometimes I was too full of myself for my own good. I left the experience humbled, and that is a good thing. I learned how difficult and emotionally draining it is to candidate for a position that you really want, and that made me a more sympathetic and sensitive provost with others who were interviewing on my campus. I learned how disappointing rejection can be, so I did my best to ensure that we responded personally and respectfully when bad news was in order. That made our institution better. And I learned that my wife had no interest whatsoever in living where there is a long cold winter with heavy accumulations of snow. That's good to know, too.

A year or so later, I was telling a friend about this experience, a college president who was surprised to learn that I would even consider leaving San Diego. That led to an offer at his institution, and it was there that our marriage became stronger and put down deep roots. It was there that my wife began to develop her gift of hospitality and gain a new vision of how she might use her gifts and graces to serve the church. And it was there that my own professional skills and character were tested in less than ideal conditions. These were all good things.

In the end, I still can't say that the three-message venture was a good experience for me, but I can say that good came from it. As I look back, as much of life can only be understood looking in that direction, I can see that this experience challenged and changed me—theologically, spiritually, professionally, and personally, and I am better for it. Lord, *open wide the eyes of my soul that I may see good in all things*. This is my prayer, today and always.

Open the Eyes of My Soul

The epigraph at the beginning of this chapter provides all of us with great encouragement, "The Lord gives sight to the blind" (Ps 146:8). Since we are all sight impaired or blind in some way or another and unaware of so many things, including spiritual things, this is a wonderful promise. We do want to live with our eyes wide open, but what are we wanting from God when we ask for the eyes of our soul to be opened? What do we mean when we refer to the eyes of our soul in the first place, and how, if at all, are these eyes connected to our physical eyes? We'll look first at spiritual sight, the eyes of the soul, before turning our attention to how we can live with our spiritual eyes wide open.

Most of us live very busy lives, too busy, if we are honest. There isn't as much time as we would wish for quiet reflection, contemplation, and retreats, the spiritual practices that we normally turn to, or at least think about, for spiritual introspection and self-examination, the activities that would help our spiritual insight—and sight. So, short of becoming a monk or a hermit, how do we gain our spiritual eyes, the eyes of the soul? I have come to believe that it starts with intentionality, a firm belief that we *can* go through the daily activities of our lives with our spiritual eyes wide open. If we are faithful to the possibility of spiritual sight and intentional about setting our hearts and minds in doing so, I truly believe that God will give sight to the blind, to us. That's the promise.

If we are careful and prayerful about seeing people as God sees them, our world opens up—the humdrum daily interactions become sacred, *all of them*, the one who pumps our gas or checks out our groceries or serves us dinner at a local restaurant. We see differently the one who delivers the mail, sweeps the office floors, and unclogs our plumbing, or the one who walks by the house each day or any of our neighbors for that matter. Even irritating interactions like telemarketers and slow drivers can be sacred, too, although I must confess that I can be very short with uninvited interruptions by salesclerks and unsolicited visits from religious and political groups who canvas the neighborhood. Honestly, I am working on my attitude and the way I react. I am not suggesting that we need to let folk who are selling something we don't want or pushing something we don't need run roughshod over us or snatch away thirty minutes of our day, but I am convinced that if God is present in every interaction we have, it does behoove all of us to treat everyone with dignity and grace, even when, and perhaps especially when, we don't want what they are selling or like what they are promoting. From time to time, we all need to be reminded that God is not only present each day in every encounter we have, God is at work in their lives, too, whether they know it or not and whether we know it or not. This makes all encounters sacred.

I would add just one additional comment about seeing people around us with spiritual eyes. Looks can be deceiving. So many of us go through the day, especially in public and in church, wearing a mask, having learned to put on a happy face in the company of strangers and friends alike. Yet, if the truth be told, many of us are lonely, anxious, broken, or scared to death. In some way or another, we are all broken pots. Learning to look behind the mask, seeing folk for who they really are and sharing who we really are, too, takes discernment, courage, and grace. What if we started each day by asking God to give us spiritual eyes to see behind the masks of those we meet, and to take off our masks, too? Since everyone on this earth has a story to tell, one of the most graceful acts we can do is to respectfully look someone in the eyes and listen without judgment or advice. If something must be said, a simple "me too" can carry the day.

When we use the eyes of our soul, our spiritual eyes, we not only see others differently, which we do, we also see successes and failures differently. We see that appearance, achievement, and affluence are not, and cannot be, the driving values in our lives. The pursuit of these values and padding our resumes will dry us up like an old leaf, demanding our time and attention while draining our spirit and energy. Rather, if we see character, community, and compassion as the values that give sight to the blind, they can guide our way. We see opportunities to serve rather than to be served, to lift others up rather than to grab for all the attention and take all the credit, to encourage others rather than to be the needy one, to be a giver rather than the taker, and to see and celebrate growth and grace in the many ordinary aspects of our lives. And as we do, we come to see that all of life is sacred, especially the ordinary moments in our own neighborhoods and in our day-to-day lives.

When we live this way, we see God at work in us and through us, and see grace all around us—in a story told in a movie or song or novel, in the joy of a child at play, in the beauty of a forest, and in the dignity and wisdom of an elder. Of course, we all want this kind of vision, so why is it so difficult to use our spiritual sight in everyday life? One reason is that we just get busy and become preoccupied with the immediate—planning meals, getting the laundry done, preparing for the next meeting, having coffee, getting the oil changed, or showing up to church on time. And we become distracted by sports, politics, the weather, or gossip to the point that we lose sight of what is happening right in front of us. The immediate dominates our attention and obstructs our view of the eternal.

At other times, we are dismissive and uninterested in those who cannot help us get what we are after, whatever that is. Relationships can easily become a means to an end. That is, if they cannot help us, we do not see them or work to maintain them. In doing so, we objectify that which is sacred. Preoccupied, distracted, dismissive, and indifferent—not a formula to see good in all things or to see clearly at all. I have come to believe that the key is to start each day with a simple prayer, asking God to give sight to the blind, to each of us. With his help, we desire to see that *all* of life is sacred, even the events of our very ordinary lives. And when we make this a priority, our vision will gradually improve. It will take time, but if we practice this spiritual discipline with prayer and intention, we will bear fruit in season, and with God's help we will begin to see good in all things—in our journeys, in all places, and at all times, even in our pain and suffering.

Seeing Good in All Things

In some aspects of our lives, it is easy to see God at work. In others, not so much. Surely we do need God's help if we desire to see good in all things. I am convinced that good can come from even the most difficult times in our lives. That is not to say that everything that happens to us is good, but what we experience, the things that come our way—the good, bad, and ugly, will change us, and as we noted earlier in this chapter, they can change us for the better. God is present and at work in all facets of our lives. Let's look with our spiritual eyes wide open for good in several of life's common experiences, starting with open and closed doors.

When doors open up for us, it is exciting and easy to see the obvious good in it. After all, we have just been admitted to grad school or offered a promotion or purchased a new house or obtained a lease for a storefront to start a new business. We have been blessed and it is natural to share the good news. Everyone loves open doors. They provide the opportunities to grow and develop and try new things. They give us a fresh start, even a chance at a new identity, and most of us are quick to give God the credit and the glory. However, sometimes open doors can go to our heads and cause spiritual amnesia if we are not careful. We can forget about who opened the doors and start thinking that we opened them on our own. I have done it myself a time or two. Part of seeing good in all things, especially the good things, is to be mindful that we never open the doors of opportunity all by ourselves and exclusively with our own skills and abilities. We always stand on the shoulders of others.

When I left home as a first-generation college student, my father, who never finished high school, looked me straight in the eyes and said, "Don't forget where you come from, son." That was wonderful advice that I have heeded to this very day. When we walk through open doors, others have paved the way and very often sacrificed some of their own dreams and opportunities on our behalf. It is good to walk through our open doors with our spiritual eyes wide open and our egos intact, expressing gratitude every chance we get. And it is also important to be mindful that an open door for us usually means a closed door or a loss for someone else. Humility is always the order of the day.

Sometimes it is a bit harder to see good when the doors close in our face. We receive a rejection notice from a grad school or a book publisher. We do not make the worship team at church. We lose an election for a spot on the board, or someone else gets the job we have worked so hard to get and dreamed about for so long. In the face of deep disappointment, I am not one to tell you to make lemonade out of lemons or that every cloud has a silver lining either. That is simply too trite to hear when the sound of a slamming door is still ringing in your ears. Some clouds are just too devastating for some sugary platitude, but I will say this—doors do close, life happens, and we have to face that reality with the faith that God is present, too, even if that reality is hard to see at the moment.

So, how do we see good in all things when we are staring at a closed door? First, we grieve and admit that we are disappointed. We do not shy away from our feelings. Rather, we own and embrace them, and shed a few tears, too—but we do not let them blind us. At some point, we must arrive at a place where we see that a closed door is not the end of the world, despite how disappointing or hurtful or embarrassing it feels at the time. We admit to ourselves that it simply was not meant to be—and we begin to move on, to knock on other doors. It all takes time and courage, but we do learn that a closed door isn't fatal, and we learn that we are never left alone to face the road ahead solely with our own wits. We are shaped by closed doors, and when a door or two opens for us, we walk through them as different persons—seeing good in all things.

Perhaps the hardest door of all is the door that is not answered at all—neither opened nor closed. There is no answer, just silence. So where is God when an answer does not come? Honestly, sometimes it is very difficult to tell, but I have come to believe that despite our doubts to the contrary, God is present and at work in the silence, too. The reasons for this silence may never be fully understood, but a silent door is an invitation to wait, watch, and listen—spiritual practices that we rarely employ when we are busy walking through an open door or grieving a closed one. It is in the silence of an unanswered door that God can speak to us in a still small voice, a voice that assures us that we are not alone, that we are bought with a price, and that God loves us dearly. It is in the silence that we can see God at work in us and around us, and we can see fingerprints of grace in our own story and in the stories of our neighbors. Even though an unanswered door is not what we pray for, it just might be the most powerful answer to prayer I know, particularly when we pray to see good in all things.

It is also difficult at times to see good in the everyday places and ordinary times of our lives, particularly because it is difficult to see God in the commonplace and daily routines of our unremarkable lives. Of course, it is easy to sense God's presence in a cathedral or along the ocean beach or in the redwood groves, but what about the grocery market, the gas station, the motor vehicle office, or the dentist? That's harder, isn't it? I know it is for me. For some reason, most of us carry the unspoken impression that God dwells only in special places: temples, cathedrals, clouds, burning bushes, and mountain tops—an understanding of God that is as old as the hills. But if we are to take Jesus' promise seriously that he will be with us *always*, even to the end of the age (Matt 28:20), that does not sound like an exclusive word to me. In fact, such a promise makes all of life sacramental. The distinction we make between the sacred and the secular is artificial. It is all sacred, even washing the dishes or doing the laundry, perhaps especially when washing the dishes or doing the laundry. God is present.

And how do we see good in terrible things, in our pain and suffering? This, of course, is much harder for all of us, but I have come to believe that even in our darkest moments, God is present—bringing strength, wisdom, peace, and love beyond imagination. I know that some will say that I am being silly here. Others will think that such a statement is simply naïve, even irresponsible. I get that, but as we look back carefully at our own lives and the lives of others, we can see that God has been with us all along, and that good has come from some of the rottenest circumstances we can imagine. Some may call this affirmation senseless, but I call it seeing good in all things through the eyes of the soul. Others will call this assertion absurd, but I call it grace. Seeing good in all things is a gift from God, bringing wisdom beyond our best insights, strength beyond our weaknesses, and hope beyond our ability to comprehend—it is grace upon grace. When we pray, "Open the eyes of my soul that I may see good in all things," we pray for a miracle, a miracle that is available to all of us regardless of the mess we are in or the difficulties we face. It has been said that grace is the great leveler, which it is, but it is also the great healer.

Scripture

Fighting the Good Fight

Just before his death, Paul wrote a second letter to his young colleague, Timothy, encouraging him to carry on the work he had started. Paul had literally poured everything he had into this ministry, and he knew that the end of his life was near. He wrote to Timothy, "I am already being poured out like a drink offering, and the time for my departure is at hand" (2 Tim 4:6). The departure he was referring to was not a departure from prison, although he would have surely welcomed such an event. No, the departure Paul meant was his departure from this world, and it was coming quickly, clearly in sight.

Paul encouraged Timothy to be faithful, to shun false doctrine, and to preach the word. As he neared the end of his instructions for Timothy, Paul could not help but reminisce a bit about the whirlwind of events he had experienced since Jesus appeared to him on the Damascus Road.

There were certainly many good times to remember—receptive audiences, new congregations, sacrificial giving and living, gracious hospitality, exciting journeys, and faithful witnesses to the inward working of Christ. But there were low times, too—he had been challenged, rejected, abused, falsely accused, mobbed, beaten, run out of town, imprisoned, and deserted at one time or another by just about everyone close to him. It was a fantastic journey of faith but it wasn't a smooth one, and some of his troubles were of his own doing. He was a lot like you and me.

As he closed his letter, Paul wanted Timothy to know this, "I have fought the good fight, I have finished the race, I have kept the faith" (2 Tim 4:7). What a wonderful testimony of faithfulness, passion, and persistence. Biblical scholars wonder if Paul meant that he had fought *a* good fight or *the* good fight. Actually, I think it was both. Paul put up a good fight as he fought the good fight—the journey of a lifetime, and he finished the race and kept the faith. I don't think his choice of the word "good" was accidental. The fight was good, all of it, including being ignored, beaten, jailed, and deserted by some of his closest friends and followers. The news of Christ was being preached, and that was good. He remained faithful to his calling, and that was good. He was able to hand the ministry baton to Timothy and a few other younger followers. They would now lead the work and move it forward. That was good, too. As Paul looked back on his life with the eyes of his soul, he saw good in all things. I doubt that he would take back any of it, even if he could.

Paul's good fight reminds me of the words of Jesus, "I have told you these things, so that in me you may have peace. In this world you will have trouble. But take heart! I have overcome the world" (John 16:33). These are good words for all of us.

Some Practical Advice

Before we conclude this chapter, I want to share four practical strategies for seeing good in all things through the eyes of the soul. To be sure, they are not earthshaking, but they are honest and helpful suggestions nonetheless when we struggle in the midst of disappointments, difficulties, and tragedies.

Be Mindful of God's Presence

One Ignatian spiritual practice is to be mindful of God's presence in the everyday and extraordinary events of our lives by simply repeating, "God is here, God is here." In the middle of a terrible argument with a loved one, a disturbing conversation with your boss, or a devastating diagnosis from your doctor, saying and remembering that "God is here, God is here, even now" adds a spiritual dimension to whatever we are experiencing, bringing comfort and assurance to our circumstance. Honestly, I really cannot tell you exactly how this simple practice works or why it is so helpful, but I assure you that it does and it is. Being mindful of God's presence invites and engages the eyes of the soul, even in the worst of situations.

Lament

Many of us carry the misconception that if we truly believe that God is with us, then we should put on a happy face and not show any anger and disappointment. That is, we should not lament—to feel, show, or express sorrow or regret. Of course, there is a long tradition of lament in Scripture. For example, there is Psalm 22:1, which Jesus quoted on the cross, "My God, my God, why have you forsaken me?" This was not a happy face expression. Rather, it was an honest response to what Jesus was experiencing at that terrible moment, and what David, the writer of the psalm, expressed before him. Even when we are confident that there is good in all things and we are determined to see it, we do not need to hide our pain and sorrow. It helps us to embrace our situation truthfully, and God and those who love us the most can take it.

It seems to me that the trouble with lament comes when we can never get past it or move on. We get stuck in the mud, and lament becomes our permanent reality, unable to see good in anything, let alone in all things. In effect, lament replaces the ditch we are in and becomes a new one, and we can't find our way home. Of course, that is not healthy either. When our spiritual eyes are wide open, we do look back and see that God has been faithful, and we look ahead to a new journey of faith. Lament is an important season, but the seasons do change.

Slow Down

A good friend and university colleague of mine was a glassblower, a true artist. It was poetry in motion to watch him work, and the beauty of his creations was absolutely stunning. I would watch him work in his glass studio for hours on end. He would also teach young apprentices to blow glass, and it was fun (and a bit amusing) to watch them work. They were nervous, of course, and their movements were neither as poetic nor their creations quite as compelling, but they were quickly learning that there was both an art and a craft to creating artistic pieces. Working with molten glass that would cool all too quickly, I heard him once tell a young student, "You only have about 40 seconds to finish this stage or you'll have to start over—so take your time!" Sometimes we get caught up in a self-imposed urgency and try to rush things to completion, all to our own detriment. Truly, haste makes waste.

So it is when we are healing and trying to see good in things that have hurt or diminished us. That takes time, too. While we are inclined to rush to get back on track and return to normal, whatever that means, the best thing we can do is to slow down, even stop, listen to God, and reflect on our experiences. I have found that journaling is a great help in this process. Writing requires us to think carefully and reflect at a writer's pace. This invites time for healing and insight, and for God to speak to us. If we sincerely want to see good in all things, it requires some inner work on our part. Journaling is a contemplative discipline that pays spiritual dividends.

Share Your Story

In addition to remaining mindful of God's presence, lamenting, and slowing down, there is one final word of practical advice that I want to share with all of us: tell your story. Stories are powerfully connective; we all relate to them in deep and personal ways. When we share our stories about seeing God in unexpected places, it gives perspective and hope for others who are traveling the same road, and it does the same for us. When we tell our stories, it lets others know that they are not the only one in the world to experience difficulties and failures, and it lets others see that good can come from even the darkest of times. In addition, when we tell our stories, it gives permission for others to honestly and courageously share their stories, too.

Conclusion

Seeing good in all things is a spiritual discipline, an act of faith and hope, the confidence in the character of God. It requires that the eyes of the soul be open to divine workings in the midst of our pain and difficulties, recognizing that all of life has a spiritual dimension, even the most mundane events of our daily lives or the most hurtful circumstances we can imagine—all of them.

We know that we *are* changed by the things we experience and by what we practice, and we *can* be changed for the better. Whether doors open wide, remain closed, or go unanswered, our confidence is in a God who goes before us and is with us, bringing hope and healing in the light of our most ordinary days or the darkest of nights. We know that life is messy, but we also know that God is faithful.

At the end of the day, we can look back and see good in all things. Not everything we encounter will be good, of course, we know that; but we also know that good can come from the worst of situations. Even in our lament we pray: "Open wide the eyes of my soul that I may see good in all things." From the stories of others and in our own stories, too, we know that God will do it.

Questions for Reflection and Discussion

1. If you were to tell a story of how you now see good coming from a very bad experience in your own life, what story would you tell?

2. Think of someone you know who needs to hear your story. How can your story best be shared?

3. Is there someone you know who needs a listening ear to tell their story? How can their story best be shared?

4. Why is it so difficult for all of us to have doors unanswered when we knock, even harder than having the doors close? Is it the frustration of not being heard, the fear of a bad result, or . . . ?

5. If all of life, even the most ordinary of events, is sacred, what can you do each day to use the eyes of your soul in partnership with your physical eyes to see and celebrate God at work?

FOR TODAY

O God:
Give me strength to live another day;
Let me not turn coward before its difficulties or prove recreant to its duties;
Let me not lose faith in other people;
Keep me sweet and sound of heart, in spite of ingratitude, treachery, or meanness;
Preserve me from minding little stings or giving them;
Help me to keep my heart clean, and to live so honestly and fearlessly that no outward failure can dishearten me or take away the joy of conscious integrity;
Open wide the eyes of my soul that I may see good in all things . . .

10

Receiving a New Vision

Guide me in your truth and teach me, for you are God my Savior . . .
—PSALM 25:5

Introduction

When we join David in asking God to guide us "in your truth and teach us" (Ps 25:5), we are embarking on a journey for wisdom's sake, to gain a new vision of God's truth. I cannot think of a more significant or sacred undertaking, and it is certainly a lifelong adventure in faith. Yet, in "For Today," we pray "grant me this day some new vision of thy truth." This day? How can a lifelong journey be achieved in a single day, this day? It doesn't quite make sense, does it? I have come to believe that wisdom's journey is actually a series of steady and reliable insights that leads us to a new point of view, a new way of seeing God at work in us and through us. It is what I call a developmental spirituality, and it can start any day, especially this day, when we earnestly pray for a new vision of the kingdom. The journey starts with a conscious recognition that there is a new vision to be had for the asking and the courage to see things as they really are instead of how we wish them to be.

In this chapter, I want to share how my vision of God's truth has changed as I have prayed, *"Grant me this day some new vision of thy truth."* As it turns out, it is one of the most profound and formative prayers I know, leading any of us on an adventure of faith and learning. Hopefully, examples of my own spiritual insights will provide discernment for your journey, too. At the end of the day, seeing God clearly comes with experience, requiring an open mind and a deep faith in the God who loves us and desires to be our ever-present teacher, guiding us into all truth.

* * *

The Boy Scout National Jamboree

By almost any measure, my boyhood days were largely ordinary. I grew up in a small town in central Michigan with three brothers in a stable and nurturing family where our primary activities involved church, school, sports, and Boy Scouts. Honestly, there was not much more to focus on, but life for me was full. I particularly loved scouting, learning to enjoy and protect our natural resources along with a variety of wilderness and life skills for doing so. It was great fun. Our troop consisted of about twenty-five to thirty boys at any one time, meeting weekly at the Boys Club, and a weekend a month for some type of outing, usually camping or hiking.

I clearly remember 1964. It was an interesting time in our nation's history—best remembered perhaps for the Beatles' appearance on the Ed Sullivan show, sandwiched between Martin Luther King's "I Have a Dream" speech in 1963 and the US entry in the Vietnam War in 1965. While most of us were smitten by the Beatles, my best memory of 1964 is the Boy Scout National Jamboree in Valley Forge. In our scout troop, the practice had been that only one or two older boys went to camp or to some other special event representing the entire troop. I never gave it much thought as to why that was so; it just was the way that things were done. That is, until Doc Knowles became the scoutmaster. One evening at our weekly meeting, Doc announced that he intended for the entire troop to go to Valley Forge for the National Jamboree—all of us. It was almost unthinkable.

He said that we would all have to do some fundraising, and he would help, too, but he had confidence that we could pull it off. And pull it off we did. Of course, most of us mowed some lawns, weeded gardens, hit up our grandparents, and even tried a bake sale or two, but the returns were paltry. Still, we faithfully turned in our fundraising efforts every week at the scout meeting. Doc Knowles counted the money and shared the total, and then announced that an anonymous donor had just given $500.

Wow! We were all amazed. Each week, we brought in our meager sums, and it would be joined by another anonymous gift. Just in time and right on schedule, enough funds came in (mostly from anonymous donors) to take the entire troop to the National Jamboree.

I can still remember the morning when the big silver bus pulled up, and twenty-eight eager boy scouts stowed their backpacks and sleeping bags below and climbed aboard, bound for Valley Forge, Pennsylvania, with a stop first in Washington, DC, for some sightseeing. Most of us had never been more than fifty miles from home. Washington, DC, was simply amazing. I had never stayed in a hotel before or ridden on an elevator or an escalator—and that was just in the lobby! We saw the White House, Congress, the Library of Congress, the monuments, the FBI, Arlington National Cemetery, Mt. Vernon, and the Smithsonian. And at least twice every day, the bus would turn a corner and Doc Knowles would announce over the PA system, "And now on your left is the Boy Scout Memorial!" At that point, we would all wildly cheer at the sculpture depicting a boy scout in full uniform walking between two allegorical figures. It was all so impressive. I was proud to be a boy scout.

And the National Jamboree was impressive, too. We camped in Valley Forge with fifty-two thousand other scouts from around the globe. The fireworks show alone was worth the trip. It literally shook the ground where we were camped. My tent mate was from Mexico City. Diego and I became close during that week, quite a feat since his English was very limited, and I did not speak Spanish at all. Still, we bonded and agreed that I should come and visit his family someday in Mexico City, an aspiration that never materialized.

To this day, it is difficult to put into words just how transformative the National Jamboree experience was for a fourteen-year-old from a little backwater town in central Michigan. I saw our nation's capital, learned a great deal of national history, obtained a larger vision for scouting and for myself, grew in my understanding and acceptance of different cultures, and even realized that folk from Ohio weren't as bad as they were made out to be during football season. They seemed just like ordinary people, too. And I came home with a vision for my life, one that extended way beyond the city limits of our town. I realized that there were things out there that beckoned me, and I promised myself that I would go, see, learn, and be a part of communities far away from home. That promise I have kept, and it all started with Doc Knowles.

In fact, it was almost all Doc Knowles, as I would find out several years later. I remarked over dinner one evening that it was sure nice for all those anonymous donors to step up and fund twenty-eight boys to go to the National Jamboree. My mom smiled and simply said, "Well, it was mostly Doc Knowles doing, really. When he announced an anonymous donation, it was usually his own gift he was reporting. He gave most of the money for the entire scout troop to go. We're really a poor community, son, and even though we all scraped together what we could, it wasn't enough for more than five or six to go, but Doc wouldn't hear of it. He made it happen for the entire troop."

That was a new vision of truth for me, too. I realized for the first time that my entire community was really quite poor. There was hardly enough to go around. That was news to me. I honestly did not know how poor we were. I thought it was natural to go from paycheck to paycheck, struggling to make ends meet, putting off that new ball glove or a vacation for another time, and wearing handmade clothes to school—even in college. I learned that sometimes someone can make a great difference in another's life when they are willing to share what they have. I have tried to practice that sort of generosity, too, whenever I see a need. I don't ever want to be selfish with anything I have. And I learned that even though I have been literally around this world, working in Papua New Guinea, Brazil, Cambodia, and across Europe, I take part of home and those early relationships and experiences with me. They are who I am, too. Yes, we were poor, but we were not impoverished. We had everything we really needed.

* * *

What a transformative vision of truth, God's truth, I believe it was, and it came as a result of a transformative experience, as many new insights do. In this chapter, we will examine the implications of praying, *Grant me this day some new vision of thy truth*. We will first look at the phrase "Grant me this day," before I share some of my own new and developing visions of God. As you will see, I have come to believe that it is through transformative experiences, relationships, personal discernment, and reading and reflection that our vision of God is shaped and formed. Ultimately, I will argue that a new vision of God's truth is essentially the pursuit of wisdom, a gift from the giver of all good things, our every-present teacher.

Grant Me This Day

In one sense, it might seem silly to pray for a new vision of God's truth, a renewed vision of God, starting today. Isn't the pursuit of wisdom a lifelong pursuit, a never-ending quest to see and know God? Of course, the answer is yes. I certainly cannot remember a time when I prayed, "Grant me this day a new vision of thy truth," which I do almost every day and have done so for almost twenty years, and woke up the very next morning much wiser, with better judgment, and able to leap tall buildings in a single bound. It simply does not work that way for most of us most of the time.

So, why pray to be granted a new vision *this day*? There are several good reasons for doing so. First, today is the only day we really have. If we desire to be on wisdom's journey, it starts with a first step. That seems obvious, but it is so easy to live one day 365 times rather than to embrace each day as a new opportunity to learn and grow. We act on our prayer for a new vision this day when we embrace where we find ourselves and what we are facing as the first step in a magnificent journey, even if what we face is lousy or downright terrible. The journey starts today if we desire to make it so.

Wouldn't it be nice if there was a GPS app that would first indicate your current location (good, bad, or otherwise) and then ask for your intended destination? All you would have to do in type in "wisdom" or "a new vision of God's truth," and the GPS would spell out the necessary steps you need to take to get there, complete with all the right and left turns, a circle-back or two, along with the length of the journey and an estimated time of arrival. And if you took a wrong turn, the voice would simply redirect your journey without recrimination or irritation. That would be nice, but that is not the way it works, is it? There is no best way or fastest route to get there and no GPS to help you, and I can tell you that there will be many twists and turns and maybe a traffic jam or two ahead. All we can do is start with an earnest intent to see God in a new way—today. If we commit to the journey and take the first step, we will begin the journey of a lifetime, even if like Abraham, we obey and go even though we do not know where we are going (Heb 11:8). If we embrace the uncertainty, we are on a new adventure of faith.

And it is important to embrace the journey, not just the destination. Have you ever traveled with someone who was hell-bent to get to that day's destination, refusing to stop for any sightseeing, places of interest, or even for a bathroom break? Yikes! It reminds me of our family vacations. My father was so intent on getting to the campsite that we never stopped for anything—not even to eat. And as it turned out, we always arrived early to our destination, but lost half the fun of getting there. At the end of the day, in many respects, the journey *is* the destination. The going and all that happens along the way is what shapes and forms us, giving us a new vision of God's truth—and of God, too. And it all starts with an intentional first step to begin the journey today.

So, we start today, this day, on a journey for a new vision of God's truth, but why do we pray for God to grant us this new vision? Are we saying that God can simply give us this new vision, not requiring our involvement? Does a new vision come from God in some sort of dramatic pronouncement from a burning bush like Moses received (Exod 3), or the result of being struck blind on the road to Damascus like Paul (Acts 9:1–19a)? I surely believe that such events have and can occur, but honestly, in my experience, they are few and far between. While I have heard God speaking directly to my spirit and into my life on an occasion or two, I have to confess that most days it doesn't happen that way, even though it would be nice if it did. It would take all of the uncertainty and my own efforts out of the equation. I could just sit back and watch as I grow in wisdom and good judgment. Perhaps that is exactly why it does not happen that way. Even while we pray for God to grant us a new vision, we must understand that we have a part to play, and it is our experiences, relationships, disappoints, and successes that provide the good soil of our lives where wisdom grows. We ask God for this gift, and it will be granted to us, but it requires our own participation, too. We have to live our lives each day with intention, praying that God will grant us a new vision as we desire and work to see and participate in God's work around us and through us. When we do, we will look back over a number of experiences, relationships, and insights, and thank God for each of them as gifts that have shaped and formed us, giving us a new vision of God's truth.

In the next section, I want to share several understandings I have come to over the years, ways that I now see God and the work of the kingdom differently. I must confess that I am a bit reluctant to share these insights since I know that not everyone will agree with my conclusions. In addition, I know that it is so easy to get sidetracked on a discussion (or argument) about the nature of truth—what is its nature, where is it found, how is it best understood, etc. . . . Of course, these are important discussions, but outside the scope of this book. As we pray for a new vision of God's truth, I will leave the meaning of the word up to each of us. What follows is simply and honestly shared as an illustration of how time and experience can shape our understanding of God. I know it has mine.

A New Vision of Thy Truth

Here are five understandings that have changed over the past fifteen years as I have earnestly prayed to be granted a new vision of God's truth, and, of course, gone through a difficult time or two. I hope these examples are helpful and illustrative of how we grow in grace and truth as we earnestly seek to know God.

First, I do not really know for sure how I came by the notion that God wanted me to empty myself of everything inside me (because it must be bad)—my desires, my thoughts, my feelings, my plans, my relationships—in order for God to fill me with his spirit, but there it is. Somehow, I thought that everything in me was vulgar and self-seeking, and must be replaced with something spiritual. In some unexplainable way, I came to believe that I was to walk around like some type of zombie, a shell of an empty person, waiting and praying to be filled with God's spirit. I now believe that God does not want me to be empty, but rather full—full of hopes, full of dreams, full of passion, full of compassion, full of ideas, full of talent, and full of love for God and neighbor. God does not want to use me like some kind of spiritual water bottle, an empty container ready to be filled with a diet drink or juice, but rather as a partner to use the gifts and graces that have been given to me to advance the kingdom. That is a major vision shift.

Second, the way I understand God's leading in my life has changed. I used to think that God had a specific plan for my life—where I went to school, what job I took, where I lived, and whom I would marry. I had to find the blueprint and follow it or I was in deep trouble. Now please hear me when I say that I do believe deeply in God's guidance and pray for it daily, but I have come to believe that God gives us a brain and talents and opportunities each day to do kingdom work. I have come to believe that God gives many more choices and freedom than I once thought possible. Instead of getting up each day asking God to direct my entire life, fearing that I might make a mistake, including the clothes I was to wear that day, I now believe that God's will is to be found and understood at the intersection of my abilities and my opportunities. To quote from Isaiah, "Whether you turn to the right or to the left, your ears will hear a voice behind you, saying, 'This is the way; walk in it'" (30:21). I have found this to be true in my own life—the voice I hear is with me, assuring me to walk in the way, *whether* I turn to the right or to the left. God says in effect, "Take your choice. I'll be with you." That is a big shift, too.

My understanding of what is sacred has changed. I used to think that ministry was sacred and all other work was secular. I used to think that the church was sacred but the world was secular (and to be avoided at all costs). The important things happened in church and in its formal ministry. The rest was just unimportant—a way to get through the week and support the ministry work on Sunday, assisted by a Wednesday evening prayer meeting to bolster our sagging spirits. Now, I see that all of life is connected in deep and mystical ways, ways that we do not even understand completely, and that all of life and work is sacred—all of it.

And this understanding that all of life is sacred gives new meaning to the commandment to love our neighbor as well as God with all our hearts, minds, and strength. Loving our neighbor or the one in the ditch is deep spiritual kingdom work. In an ultimate sense, it is all ministry. I have also come to see that the command to love our neighbors as ourselves can be taken quite literally. Of course, many love to go on mission trips to some far-off, isolated areas of the world for ministry, to love our neighbors there. While I have no particular axe to grind about these activities, I will say that it is easy to gravitate to such activities as the best way to love our neighbors. In fact, our churches give so much time and attention to these activities that it is easy to conclude that it is the only way to love our neighbors. Neighbors must live far away. I have come to believe that we can take this commandment quite literally. Our neighbors are the ones who actually live near us, even next door. We are commanded to love them as we love ourselves, even if they have an irritating barking dog or don't mow their lawn as often as we do.

Finally, I have come to believe that in the last analysis, it is the quality of our relationships that count—our relationship with God, with our neighbors, our friends, our families, even with ourselves. It is not the list of accomplishments on our resumes that make any real difference or have any ultimate meaning, but rather the memories and influence of our relationships. It is through our relationships that we see and share in the life of Christ.

Over the last fifteen years, I have asked God to grant me a new spiritual vision. That request has been granted, sometimes through a new insight but more often than not through my experiences (many difficult), genuine relationships, and time. I now focus less on judgment and more on love; less on right belief and more on formative practice; less on high-profile ministry activities and more on loving those who live in my own neighborhood, and less on gaining attention and notoriety and more on being the kind of friend someone would call when they end up in the ditch. I trust that God will continue to shape and guide me as I pray each day, *Grant me this day some new vision of thy truth.*

Scripture

The Jews were looking for the messiah to come, someone who would lead a rebellion, drive out the Romans and their other oppressors, and establish a Jewish kingdom again in Jerusalem. The Jews detested the Romans, at least in part because the Jews were required by law to carry a Roman soldier's gear for a mile if asked, immediately dropping everything they were doing and complying with the order. No questions asked. Of course, they had no choice but to do so submissively, but under their breath they whispered, "When the messiah comes, we'll see who carries whose gear then!" They wanted the messiah to set things right—and the sooner the better.

And Jesus himself talked and taught a good deal about the coming kingdom—his kingdom, and even taught his disciples to pray that the kingdom would come. In fact, the gospels report that Jesus mentioned the kingdom of God at least twenty-six times, but there was a huge disconnect between what Jesus was trying to say and what the Jews, even his disciples, perhaps especially his disciples, wanted to hear. They wanted their king to sit on the throne in Jerusalem, a sovereign ruling over the entire world with Rome as a footstool.

However, Jesus was quite clear that he was a messiah of another kind. During the sermon on the mount, Jesus told the listeners that when someone makes you carry his pack one mile, carry it a second mile (Matt 5:41). This, of course, was not what anyone wanted to hear. Even John the Baptist from a prison cell sent several of his followers to ask his cousin: Are you the one or should we look for another? Now John clearly knew about Jesus' divine mission, but in essence he was asking,

"Are you going to do this or not? Where is your army? When does the battle start? Let's get on with it!" Jesus told his questioners to go back and report to John that the sick were being healed, the lame were walking, and the blind were seeing again. While these signs showed Jesus' majesty and power, this was clearly not what John had in mind for the messiah (Matt 11:2–5; Luke 7:18–22). And when Jesus told his disciples that tough times were ahead, they announced defiantly that they had two swords. "'That's enough!' he replied" (Luke 22:38). Clearly there would be no army. Soon thereafter, before Pontius Pilate, Jesus told all who would listen, "My kingdom is not of this world" (John 18:36a). And after his resurrection, Jesus kept teaching about the kingdom, telling Peter to "feed my sheep" (John 21:17). Obviously, feeding the sheep and caring for the lambs was totally different from raising up an army in revolt.

The kingdom had come, but so many didn't even see it, although it was staring them right in the face. Why? I believe that the answer, at least in part, lies in the fact that even those closest to Jesus could not get past their own preconceived notions about who Jesus was supposed to be, how he was to go about his ministry, and what he was supposed to do for them. Rather than listening and following Jesus, they were eager to make the messiah in the image of their own expectations, to serve their own desires and dreams. They did not listen; instead they projected and dictated, and in doing so, they couldn't see the truth because they only saw what they wanted to see.

There is a lesson here for all of us. When we pray, *Grant me this day some new vision of thy truth*, we must be clear that it is a new vision of *thy* truth that we are after and not a confirmation of *my* truth. It is a profound spiritual undertaking to seek a new vision of who God is rather than who we want God to be. We start by letting God speak to us rather than trying to dictate to God. The beginning of wisdom, I have come to believe, is to let God be God, full of mystery, wonder, grace, and truth.

Some Practical Advice

Before we conclude this chapter, I want to offer all of us several words of practical advice as we seek a new vision of God's truth. There are four virtues that come into play if we are sincere about this quest for spiritual wisdom. The first is humility, the humility to recognize and admit that we do not have all the answers. In fact, we do not even know all the questions. This is a good place to start—with the humble admission that there is much more for us to learn—that we don't know it all, and asking the right, even troubling, questions is more important than having all the answers fit nicely into our own worldview. In fact, we have to admit that we will never have all the answers—we're not God. We join the Apostle Paul in confessing that we only see a reflection in the mirror and know only in part (1 Cor 13:12). The path to wisdom, I have come to believe, begins with humility.

And hospitality and humility go hand in hand, like two sides of the same coin. If we first admit that we do not have everything figured out, it opens us up to graciously welcome other points of view and ways to see God's work in this world, and in our own lives, too. It is through the practice of hospitality, in breaking bread together (figuratively and literally), and in listening carefully and thoughtfully to others who see things differently without the need to challenge their ideas or correct their theology, that offers a generative opportunity to grow in wisdom and grace.

Along with the practice of humility and hospitality, a third virtue is required of us—courage, the courage to admit that our own view of God's truth may not only be limited, which it surely is, but also that it might be wrong, or at least terribly incomplete. It always takes the rawest kind of courage to admit that we may have it wrong, yet a new vision of God's truth requires that we be humble about what we do not know, open and gracious to other views of how God works, courageous enough to admit that we may be wrong, and honest enough to concede when we are.

Finally, gaining a new vision of God's truth takes patience. It is not something that just springs up overnight. The pursuit of wisdom takes time. New insights usually come when we reflect back on our journey—particularly to times when we were in the ditch or we walked with someone who was or still is. It is certainly a mystery how the road to wisdom stretches out both before us and behind us, but in some profound way, we walk both ways. As we look forward to growth and wisdom, it is often by looking back on the roads we have traveled that gives us the confidence and courage to move forward. We will address this dynamic a bit more in the next chapter. Suffice it here to say that we grow in wisdom and grace more through our difficulties than by our successes; more through the times and events in our lives when we are hurt and afraid and lonely than when we are popular and proud; and more when we have to eat some crow than when we have much to crow about. If we take this prayer seriously, asking for a new vision of thy (God's) truth, it demands that we practice humility, hospitality, courage, and patience. At the end of the day, the pursuit of wisdom is gratifying, but not for the faint of heart.

Conclusion

"For Today," the prayer we have been praying and contemplating together in this book, begins as a prayer of desperation, *Oh God, give me strength to live another day*. It is a prayer when we are in the ditch and at our wits end. We are not even sure how to pray. All we have strength to do is to ask for divine assistance to make it through the day. It is a prayer that most of us have prayed on more than one occasion. Some of us are praying such a prayer even now.

About half-way through, however, the prayer shifts from desperation to anticipation. It turns into a request for spiritual growth and insight—help me to keep my heart clean, open the eyes of my soul so I may see good in all things, and as we have examined in this chapter, please grant me a new vision of thy truth. These are prayers with the expectation that better days are ahead of us. We are out of the ditch and moving on down the road. Finally, we have something in mind other than to just get home before dark. As we have discussed, the desire to grow in wisdom and knowledge begins any day we decide to sincerely and intentionally start the journey, but humility, hospitality, honesty, and courage must guide us or we will end up right back where we began. And since it is a journey of many steps, patience and persistence are needed, too.

As I have tried to make clear, it is through transformative experiences (tough times, even tragic ones), trusted relationships, personal discernment, and careful reading and reflection that our vision of God is shaped and formed. Yes, it is a journey of many steps, often only fully understood when we look back and reflect on God's faithfulness to us, even when we were at our worst, perhaps especially when we were at our worst. When we aspire to a new vision of God's truth, the more this becomes clear: life is messy, but God is faithful—the ever-present teacher to all who desire to learn more about him, grow closer to him, and become more like him.

Questions for Reflection and Discussion

1. Can you look back on a particularly difficult time in your life and see how it shaped your vision of the character of God?

2. Do you have a trusted friend or group where you would feel comfortable sharing your deepest fears and wildest questions, even about God? Would you say that you are such a friend for someone else? If not, how could you start to develop such a relationship?

3. Has your idea of God changed in the past decade? If so, how would you describe this journey? What would be some of the markers along the way?

4. As you reflect on the shifts that I shared in my own vision of God's truth, are there any with which you particularly agree or take exception? Why?

5. Can you point to a person or two who were key in your own spiritual development? (For me, Doc Knowles was one.) Is it too late to go back and thank them for their investment in your life? In any case, how could you pay forward their investment in you?

FOR TODAY

O God:
Give me strength to live another day;
Let me not turn coward before its difficulties or prove recreant to its duties;
Let me not lose faith in other people;
Keep me sweet and sound of heart, in spite of ingratitude, treachery, or meanness;
Preserve me from minding little stings or giving them;
Help me to keep my heart clean, and to live so honestly and fearlessly that no outward failure can dishearten me or take away the joy of conscious integrity;
Open wide the eyes of my soul that I may see good in all things;
Grant me this day some new vision of thy truth . . .

11

Regaining the Spirit of Joy and Gladness

> Joy is the infallible sign of the presence of God.
> —PIERRE TEILHARD DE CHARDIN

Introduction

On Easter Sunday, I made an unplanned visit to the emergency room at our local hospital, complaining of severe abdominal pain, which turned out to be a bout with gall stones and pancreatitis. Two surgeries and a week later, I walked out of the hospital and returned home. I was *so* happy. It was not the kind of joy and gladness that one feels when seeing the redwoods or the Grand Canyon for the first time, or the giddy kind of joy and gladness of a child when opening presents at a birthday party or Christmas. No, it was a bit different from that, deeper than that. There wasn't any whooping and hollering, but there was a genuine sense of joy and gratitude to be home, to have made it through the ordeal.

While recovering at home, my wife and I had several opportunities to reflect back over the events of the past week, and over the time we have lived in Newberg, too. I came in the summer of 2008 to serve as provost at the university. To be honest, even though I believed, and still believe, that I was at the top of my game, an experienced professional ready to do my very best work, it just did not work out that way. What was supposed to be the crowning jewel in my professional career turned out to be tough sledding from the get-go.

Two events stand out in particular. Soon after I arrived, we started planning in earnest to start a Doctor of Physical Therapy (DPT) program. There was only one other such program in the entire state of Oregon, and it was a solid mission-fit for a Christian university desiring to prepare students to serve our neighbors. We knew it would be difficult to find a qualified director and faculty, and the initial accreditation process would be a major hurdle. Still, we moved ahead faithfully, filling our staff and recruiting a full class of very bright and committed students. All we had to do was to gain initial approval from the accrediting body and we were on our way. Even though we received good reports from our own consultants and a site visitor from the accrediting body, our initial application was turned down in mid-May. We were shocked. We were supposed to start in August—and had already included nearly $750,000 in revenue from the new program in the annual budget. Of course, this was an unexpected surprise to us and a public embarrassment, too, and it meant that I would have to make massive cuts in the academic budget to account for the shortfall, including canceling all faculty development and travel support for the entire year.

No one was happy, but there was a provision to appeal the decision. So, we informed the accreditation group of our desire to appeal, and set out over the summer to write a second accreditation report and prepare for a team visit in early August. We worked on the report every single day, foregoing holidays, vacations, and family celebrations. By August, we were totally exhausted, but ready for the site visit. Imagine our joy and gladness when the chair of the site visit team called us from the airport and told us that we had done such laudatory work that our appeal had been granted on the spot. We could start right away. Of course, we did do some whooping and hollering then, but there was also a deep accompanying sense of joy and gladness that we kept working in spite of the disappointment and embarrassment. We made it, and we were quick to thank God for strength, wisdom, patience, and faith as we pressed forward in the face of a professional disaster. We were never alone, and I think we actually did better work than we were capable of doing. That is grace in action.

The other event my wife and I reminisced about during my recuperation from surgery was my last year as provost and my first year teaching in the School of Education. As I mentioned earlier in chapter 8, things were not going well for me. I had difficulty building an effective team, fitting into the executive team, leading the faculty, or pleasing my boss—certainly not the hallmarks for a successful run as provost. I tried with all my strength to turn things around, but I slowly came to realize that I needed to step down from my position. I had been successful my entire career, and I could not imagine just giving in and walking away. Surely, I kept telling myself, things will get better, but they didn't. In fact, they got worse. My last year as provost was simply awful, filled with pain and discouragement, so the boss and I agreed that I would resign my position and join the faculty as a professor in our educational leadership program. The irony of this move did not escape me. The failed leader would now teach leadership. It was necessary, but hard to swallow.

After a forty-year administrative career, I had to learn to teach all over again, and many of the courses were online. Honestly, I was afraid that I would fail again, but thankfully this assignment proved to be life-giving. I learned that I could teach effectively and serve as a supportive colleague in the department. And above all, I fell in love with our students as I walked with them through many celebrations and difficulties during their studies. And I had the opportunity to discover that I could write, and I loved doing so. Clearly, if I had not changed positions, you would not be reading this book. What started out in a sense of failure turned out to be the most rewarding job I have ever had. I would not go back to administrative work if they doubled my salary. I have some scars and some painful memories still, but I made it home.

As we reminisced about these experiences, it became clear to us that as we looked back at these difficult and painful times, we did make it. At one point, we were in the ditch, crying out to God, "Give me strength to live another day." Now, we are out of the ditch and on down the road, and we are able to look back on these tough times with a spirit of joy and gladness. In fact, in some spiritually significant way, the tough times gave us a spirit of joy and gladness. It isn't that we would ever wish to experience them again. No, we do not look back at these events with sentimentality, but we do see God's fingerprints all over our journey, bringing hope and healing and a deep contentment. Difficulties will change you, and hopefully for the better. God set a table for us in the middle of the battle, to paraphrase King David (Ps 23:5). It was a feast fit for a king.

In this chapter, we will be praying together, "Inspire me with the spirit of joy and gladness." We will examine together what it means to have a sense of joy and gladness that goes deeper than just acting happy and telling good jokes. As it turns out, the spirit of joy and gladness starts with perspective, gratitude, and contentment, and leads to humility, grace, and service.

Perspective

One thing you rarely have when you are struggling in the ditches of life is perspective. That is to say, it is hard to step back and see the big picture when you are barely keeping your head above water. You can't even move much, let alone see the road! At this point, all you want to do is survive the day and get home before dark, and the nights can be long and lonely, too. All you know to say and all you can pray is "Help!" Honestly, that is a powerful prayer—a prayer eastered up in desperation, hoping beyond hope for hope and help. It is tough business, sometimes simply awful.

But over time, it is possible to get some distance from even the most traumatic events—the loss of a loved one, a failed relationship, a business disaster, a church collapse, or the loss of a job. Of course, there are many more, but I think you get the idea. The good news is that with time, the spirit you lost in the ditch can be recovered, healing does occur. I do not mean that all the memories will go away and life will return to just how it was before. No, that is simply not possible. There will be a new normal, but the pain will subside and there will be a time when you can look back and see some good that happened even in the midst of the most heartbreaking events. Time is the great healer; healing and perspective do come.

I believe that this kind of perspective is a form of wisdom, a spiritual insight, that is able to look back into our worst moments and beyond our worst moments to understand and appreciate the reality that we are no longer in the ditch. Even though the scars, regrets, and memories come and go, there is a deep comfort that wells up with the recognition that we made it out of the ditch, and healing has and continues to occur. It is the kind of perspective that percolates up from deep within your spirit, and you say out loud, "Made it." It is the spirit of joy and gladness.

Gratitude

With some distance and healing from being in the ditch comes a realization that we were never alone, no matter how lonely we felt, and that some good has come out of the mess. Not that we wished for the ditch experience or would ever want to walk that path again, but there is a recognition that we are different persons than before. Difficulties do change us, and it is possible to get back on the road as different, more sensitive, more compassionate persons. We have a new perspective on other difficulties that we may face, and for those who face their own brand of troubles. The best way I can describe it is to say that once out of the ditch, there is a profound gratitude for the faithfulness of God and the few friends who stuck with us. We understand in a new way that we never go it alone—life is a communal act.

Contentment

A new perspective on the good that has happened in our lives, along with a deep appreciation for the way our experiences have changed us and the few who faithfully walked the path with us, feeds our souls. We find the spirit of joy and gladness welling up from within. When we pray for God to inspire us with a spirit of joy and gladness, this is what bubbles up—a deep contentment that is difficult to imagine, almost impossible to put into words, and easily misunderstood, but so very real. As we look back on all the roads we have traveled and all the ditches we have negotiated, we can affirm: *Life is messy but God is faithful.* It is the surest sign of contentment that I know, and it flows from the spirit of joy and gladness that can inspire even the most cynical and downtrodden among us.

Humility

In addition to perspective, gratitude, and contentment, the ditches of life shape us in one other important way—failure invites humility. That is to say, failures have the power to shape us in good ways far more than our successes. It is not that we cannot learn from our successes, but honestly, we usually do not. Failures, tragedies, and difficulties tend to strip away our pretenses and give space for reflection and prayer. When we are on top of the heap, we rarely have time for growth and renewal. We are too busy congratulating ourselves and planning our next victory party. Failures and difficulties of all kinds are lonely experiences, so they give time and space that lead to introspection, self-examination, and prayer, and these can lead to perspective, gratitude, contentment, and humility.

When we pray to be inspired with the spirit of joy and gladness, it is these sustaining virtues that come to the fore. Surely joy and gladness are expressions of happiness, but they are much more than simple surface emotions. They are grounded expressions of a spirited confidence in a God who would not leave us to deal with our troubles by ourselves, even those of our own doing, perhaps especially those of our own doing. As we look back, we can see that God has been, is, and always will be faithful to us. How else can such an insight be received and appreciated other than with the spirit of joy and gladness? May it be so in our lives.

* * *

Actually, there is one additional outcome that flows from the spirit of joy and gladness—compassion. As we gain appreciation and insight about our own journeys, we become less judgmental of others when they end up in the ditch. We are more inclined to say, "Me, too," and offer grace rather than judgment and unsolicited advice. Ultimately, we desire to use our own experiences—good, bad, and ugly—to be the cup of strength for suffering souls. That is the focus of the next and final chapter of this book.

Scripture

Before I offer some words of practical advice and some questions for reflection and discussion, I want us to look at several passages from Scripture that express the spirit of joy and gladness. Simple stories can teach us so much if we have ears to hear and eyes to see.

Just a Pile of Stones?

When Joshua led the nation of Israel across the Jordan River on dry ground, he instructed one member from each of the twelve tribes to go back into the riverbed, shoulder a stone, and carry it out. We pick up the story a few days later:

> One the tenth day of the first month the people went up from the Jordan and camped at Gilgal on the eastern border of Jericho. And Joshua set up at Gilgal the twelve stones they had taken out of the Jordan. He said to the Israelites, "In the future when your descendants ask their parents, 'What do these stones

mean?' tell them, 'Israel crossed the Jordan on dry ground.' For the Lord your God dried up the Jordan before you until you had crossed the river. The Lord your God did to the Jordan what he had done to the Red Sea when he dried it up before us until we had crossed over" (Josh 4:19–23).

This was no ordinary pile of stones. They were to serve as a reminder of God's faithfulness to his people, how the Israelites crossed the Jordan River on dry ground *in the same way* they crossed the Red Sea. When their children and their children's children asked about the significance of the pile of stones, they were to tell the story again. The stone pile served as an ancient memory stick.

Artifacts have a way of conveying and retaining meaning for us. I have a clock on my desk that my father made in his woodshop some years ago. Every time I look at the clock, I remember him and his love for woodworking—and for his sons, too. It is more than just a clock; it is a reminder of my heritage, and that brings me joy.

What artifacts and memories do you have on display or keep in a special place? Young children may look at them and ask, "What is that or why do you keep that here?" Just go ahead and tell them with a smile of joy and gladness. Life is messy, but God is faithful.

Peter before the Sanhedrin

Peter and John were walking to the temple one day when they were asked by a beggar at the gate for some money. They did not have any coins to throw on his dirty, worn-out blanket. Instead, they healed him on the spot, causing the beggar to rejoice and giving Peter the opportunity to preach about Jesus to a shocked but curious crowd of onlookers. This led to their arrest. The next day, Peter and John appeared before the Sanhedrin, the city council, of sorts, to be questioned. Their response to the interrogation was so powerful that "when they saw the courage of Peter and John and realized that they were unschooled, ordinary men, they were astonished and they took note that these men had been with Jesus" (Acts 4:13).

What a change! Is this the same Peter who denied even knowing Jesus three time on the night of his arrest and ran away? Wow! Of course, I am sure that there are many explanations for this turnaround, but I cannot help thinking that Peter was able to look back at his own failures and shortcomings and see God's hand upon him and his faithfulness to him. He had a new perspective now that he was out of the ditch, and a renewed sense of gratitude that translated into compassion and courage. While the text does not comment on their countenances, I have a feeling that they were inspired by the spirit of joy and gladness, and their faces clearly showed it. They may have been unschooled, ordinary men, but the spirit that flowed from deep inside them was anything but ordinary. There was an extraordinary sense of contentment in doing what they felt called to do, knowing that they would never be left alone.

* * *

I really do not think I need to connect all the dots here. These stories speak for themselves. Suffice it here to say that the spirit of joy and gladness is much more than simply and simplistically acting happy, happy, happy all the time. It springs from the knowledge that God has been with us through the most difficult of circumstances, and always will be. We made it out of the ditch, and the spirit of joy and gladness easters up from within.

Some Practical Advice

Before we conclude this chapter, let me share with you some practical advice, ways that we can recognize and cultivate the spirit of joy and gladness in our own lives. The first thing I would suggest is that you make your own pile of stones. That is to say, gather and display at least three artifacts in a location that you will see on a regular basis as a reminder of God's faithfulness to you. On my desk, in addition to my father's handmade clock, I have a small jar of marbles that my great grandfather made out of clay when he was a boy, an arrowhead that my grandfather found in a field on the family farm while planting white beans, and a Petoskey stone that I found on the shores of Lake Michigan near Traverse City while on a family vacation. These artifacts remind me of my family heritage, their deep faith in God, and the many good times I had with them. They always invoke in me the spirit of joy and gladness.

The second word of advice is this: intentionally take time to remember and reflect back on some of the ditches you have had to navigate, and recognize how God and a close friend or two helped you through the mess. If you can, stop and say "thank you" to them. Honestly, you cannot say it often enough. Expressions of appreciation mean a great deal to others, even if they act embarrassed to receive it, and it does something to you, too. I have come to believe that our humility is shaped by the simple act of saying "Thank you." Try it.

The final piece of advice is to tell your story, sharing your experience with God's faithfulness in the worst of difficulties, and if the difficulties were of your own doing, share that, too. Bearing witness to our own failings and God's presence and healing gives hope to those who are struggling—and that is most of us. And ask others to share their stories, too—listen—be a reporter—ask questions. Everyone has a story to tell, everyone. Just one or two thoughtful, sincere questions can open up the floodgates. I truly believe that one of the best ways to love our neighbors is to simply listen to them, and add a word of encouragement at the end. Most times, that will be sufficient. One of the most profound acts of personal ministry I know is to listen others into speech.

Conclusion

In this chapter, we explored what it means when we ask God to "inspire me with the spirit of joy and gladness." We started out with the recognition that the spirit of joy and gladness is not to be confused with simply being happy. Of course, there is nothing wrong with acting happy, but the spirit of joy and gladness we are seeking here is much deeper than a surface emotion and a plastic smile. It wells up from a deep sense of contentment that stems from looking back over our spiritual journey and recognizing God's faithfulness to us, even in the most difficult of situations of our own making. It also brings a sense of gratitude, humility, and compassion, qualities that enable us to help others who are in the ditch.

Through two stories from the Bible and some words of practical advice, we were encouraged to create our own pile of stones, artifacts that remind us of God's faithfulness during difficult times, and to be ready to share our own stories with others. Encouragement seems to be always in short supply. And we ended by acknowledging that the most powerful act of ministry we have at our disposal may be to simply listen to others as they tell their stories. Everyone has one, and all it takes is a well-placed question or two along with the wisdom to listen rather than to drive the conversation.

At the end of the day, the spirit of joy and gladness comes from deep within, and while it may take some intentional effort on our part to recognize and share it, this spirit comes to us as a gift from the one who prepared a table for us in the midst of our enemies. All we have to do is come and dine, and invite other suffering souls to the table, too.

Questions for Reflection and Discussion

1. Do you have some artifacts on display? If not, and you were to gather some remembrance stones, what would be your top three? Where can you place them as a constant reminder of God's faithfulness to you?

2. As you think about your remembrance stones, what is the deep, underlying message that they communicate to you?

3. Is there someone you want to thank for the way they have walked with you in difficult times? How could you convey your gratefulness to them in a unique or memorable way? Hint: breaking bread together is a spiritual act, and fun, too.

4. What is the best way for you to tell your story to others—a blog, a sermon, a story, a work of art, a poem, a song . . . ? Could this be a project that you intentionally take on over the next month?

5. Do you know someone who has a story to tell? How could you listen them into speech? What would be the priming questions you ask?

FOR TODAY

O God:
Give me strength to live another day;
Let me not turn coward before its difficulties or prove recreant to its duties;
Let me not lose faith in other people;
Keep me sweet and sound of heart, in spite of ingratitude, treachery, or meanness;
Preserve me from minding little stings or giving them;
Help me to keep my heart clean, and to live so honestly and fearlessly that no outward failure can dishearten me or take away the joy of conscious integrity;

Open wide the eyes of my soul that I may see good in all things;
Grant me this day some new vision of thy truth;
Inspire me with the spirit of joy and gladness . . .

12

Being the Cup of Strength to Suffering Souls

> A fall into the ditch makes you wiser.
> —CHINESE PROVERB

Introduction

Near the end of "For Today," we encounter this line: *And make me the cup of strength to suffering souls.* This is the major pivot in the prayer, reorienting the spiritual focus from our own difficulties to the difficulties of others. Certainly, this is a long way from where we began our journey together: *O God: Give me strength to live another day*. We started out in the ditch, and after getting back on our spiritual feet and gaining a new, albeit hard-earned, perspective, and hopefully some wisdom, too, we resume our journey down the road, hoping to be of help to other suffering souls.

In this line of the prayer, we are asking God to grant us the privilege of being the cup of strength for others in need. In a sense, this is the full circle of community. What we learn from our own difficulties and tragedies enables us to stand as witnesses that swimming in deep water and drowning are not the same thing, to paraphrase James Baldwin. In fact, to give back in some substantive way, I have come to believe, is a spiritual obligation, a summons for each of us. It is truly what it means to love our neighbors, to willingly share the wisdom we have gained and the grace that has been so freely extended to each of us.

In this final chapter, we will look closely at the desire to help others in need, what resources we have that can be helpful, and how to wisely use the wisdom and experience we have to help other suffering souls without ending up back in the ditch ourselves. But first, I want to share one final story.

In the Ditch

A friend of mine, just about my age, was a leader of a prominent organization affiliated with a strong and vibrant denomination. He was known literally throughout the church and around the globe, a bigger-than-life personality recognized for charisma, boldness, and innovation. He was an eloquent and witty public speaker, an engaging pulpiteer, and a spiritual role model for many in his organization. He was on the top of his game, and he knew it—and enjoyed it.

His career came crashing down suddenly when it was announced that he had resigned his position, forced out actually, ostensibly to spend more time with his family. He would spend the next year or so trying to figure out what happened and how to piece together his shattered career. He went from traveling a high-profile road directly into the ditch, and the fall was both sudden and sad. There were whispers of an inappropriate relationship and a cover-up, which accompanied by some very poor organizational decisions and the abuse of his power, cost him his job, perhaps his career, too. Although some of the facts were in dispute, the result was a sudden dismissal, a fall from grace, and a personal tragedy.

I immediately contacted my friend and we arranged to meet several weeks later. He said that he was fine, that it was all the fault of others, and that he would be okay in a month or two. Reflecting back on my own experience, I affirmed our friendship and cautiously did my best to convey to him that it was okay to not be okay, and while hope and healing would come, it likely would not be in the next month or two. He was in the ditch, and the journey out and on down the road looked daunting from that view, but the first steps were to ask God for help, recognize that he was in the ditch, take responsibility for the part he played in this tragedy, and find a spiritual director, mentor, or small group of trusted souls with whom he could laugh, cry, question, think, and pray. It was not good for him to be alone, and the same held for his family. They were in crisis, too.

And I also cautioned that although he was a well-known public personality with hundreds of friends and contacts, he would quickly become invisible, able to count those who would walk with him on one hand. Some simply do not know what to say, fearing that they may make matters worse. Others curiously drive by the house fire, but will not even consider stopping to help since it is not their business. He smiled and acknowledged that that had already happened. In a month since his resignation, I was only the second person to reach out to him. Sad, but typical.

We met several additional times and keep in contact via email. I am happy to report that my friend is making his way, although it has taken much more time, personal effort, and humility than he ever realized. This is almost always the case.

* * *

I am convinced that when we end up in the ditch, we go through many of the stages of grief—denial, anger, bargaining, depression, and acceptance. Healing and restoration will come, but for most of us, it takes years, not a month or two. Hopefully, the experience we go through, even if it is of our own doing, will ultimately bring some wisdom and the desire to be the cup of strength to other suffering souls.

Before we look at several stories from Scripture involving encounters of one kind or another that lend insight for our work with others and offer some words of practical advice, I want us to look at three realities we must embrace when we desire to be the cup of strength to suffering souls. As you will see, we have a key part to play, but we cannot play the hero. It does not work that way.

You Cannot Change the Entire World

When we desire to be the cup of strength for suffering souls, we must be mindful that we cannot be the cup of strength for *every* suffering soul. Our mission is not to change the entire world, but to invest in the lives of those around us. As far as I know, the world has really changed dramatically only two or three times since creation. Certainly, Jesus changed the world for all of us, but we are not Jesus. We are not called to be the savior of the world. Instead, we are asking God to make us the cup of strength to suffering souls. This is not a prayer for sainthood; it is the call to servanthood, to love our neighbors.

But we have so many neighbors, so where do we start? It can be overwhelming when we take the time to look at the needs around us, even in our own neighborhoods and communities. Begin by asking God for direction and guidance, for focus; to give us a heart for something specific and the opportunity to be involved. Rather than carrying a heavy burden for world hunger, take a prayerful and careful look at those who are hungry in your own community and what is being done to help them. I have come to believe that spending two hours a week volunteering at a local food bank is just as spiritual, perhaps more so, than spending two hours a week beseeching God to feed the hungry around the world. We hear often that it is important to find your voice—the things you care about. Of course, this is true, but it is also important to find your particular place of service. Sometimes our desire to be the cup of strength to suffering souls speaks the loudest when we jump in and lend a hand, and let our actions do the talking.

You Cannot Fix Everything

Even when we are prayerfully selective about the needs around us and who in the ditch we reach out to help, it is important to remember what we can and what we cannot do. We cannot make difficulties just go away. It is not our calling to fix everything—to fly in and save the circus. That is not our role. Our role is to be a cup of strength, an encourager and fellow traveler who helps those in the ditch recover and get back on the road. We cannot make the ditch simply go away. It is real, and there is little that we can do about that. We can, however, be available, honest, and wise. After all, we have been in the ditch, too, so there are things that we can offer to someone who is suffering—primarily our presence. One thing we should not offer, however, is unwanted and unsolicited advice, as tempting and satisfying as it may be to give it. Part of growing in wisdom is the understanding of when to speak and when to be silent—being trustworthy, faithful, and patient with a suffering soul. There is a point of readiness that someone must reach before they will listen and take to heart what we have to say, as wise as we may be. Until then, it will literally go in one ear and out the other.

You Have to Let the Healing Process Work

Grief therapists tell us that when we encounter a traumatic event like a terminal illness or the sudden loss of a loved one, we go through a rather predictable five-stage process: denial, anger, bargaining, depression, and acceptance. There is no good way to skip a step or hurry through the process. Grief will proceed at its own internal pace. I have seen stages of this process at work in less traumatic events, too, like the loss of a job, the demise of a business venture, or a public failure, even divorce. Remember the story of my friend who was forced from a high-profile job. He first responded that everything was okay—he was fine (denial), then blamed others for his problems (anger), threatened to sue (bargaining), and went into isolation (depression) before coming to own what happened and the part he played in the loss of his job and the demise of his career (acceptance). It was at that juncture that he first began to move toward a new normal.

When we are walking with a suffering soul, it is helpful to understand and expect this process to play itself out. Of course, not everyone will necessarily go through each stage, and not everyone will experience and express them in exactly the same way. Still, helping someone in the ditch make some sense of what they will or are experiencing is truly a gift. Anger, for instance, is often a necessary stage in the healing process. If it comes, let the person be angry. It is not helpful for anger to be ignored or spiritualized away with a trite saying.

When attempting to be the cup of strength to suffering souls, it is also important to keep a friendly distance. That is to say, be careful not to take on their suffering or make their pain your own. It will not help them and it will hurt you. All of this requires conscious self-care, attending to your own well-being and the activities that fill your spiritual cup. When we ask God to make us a cup of strength to suffering souls, we must always be conscious of the fact that we serve out of the overflow of our lives, so we must find ways to replenish our own spiritual cup daily. If we do not, we will soon end up in a ditch of our own, begging for water, too. Clearly, this is not a prescription for effective ministry at any level. If we are to care for others, we first have to be sure to care for ourselves.

Scripture

I want us to look briefly at two stories, one from the New Testament and one from the Old Testament; one that will be quite familiar to most of us and one that is a bit more obscure. However, both stories provide some insight to all of us who desire to be the cup of strength to suffering souls. First, the lesser-known story.

Joshua Meets the Commander of the Lord's Army

One evening, after crossing the Jordan River and just before the battle of Jericho was about to commence, Joshua looked up and saw a man standing in front of him with a drawn sword in his hand. Apparently not shaken by this, Joshua simply went up to him and directly asked, "Are you for us or for our enemies?" (Josh 5:13). You see, Joshua was in full battle mode, so when someone approached, the question was—friend or foe? However, the stranger, who turned out to be the commander of the army of the Lord, simply replied, "Neither" (5:14a). What an interesting response.

In the midst of a battle, it is natural to see everything and everyone in terms of sides—our side or their side. You are either with me or against me. Everyone has to be on one side or the other—there is no middle ground. When we attempt to be the cup of strength to suffering souls, to those in the ditch, it is easy to be pulled into battle mode, too. In essence, we are asked, "Are you for me or for my enemies. Are you with me or with them?" And we can be dragged into some very bitter conflicts as a result. That is why the commander's response is so insightful and valuable. "Neither" was his response. And that can be our response, too. Do not take sides. Be present, be faithful, be honest, but do not take sides. When we do, it is a sure bet that we will lose perspective and end up carrying some unnecessary anger ourselves, and that will not be helpful to anyone. We can be supportive without taking in the entire emotional landscape. Our reserve and perspective will promote the healing process far more than stoking an already burning flame.

Lazarus

The Gospel of John tells the remarkable story of Jesus raising Lazarus from the dead. Lazarus, a good friend, had been dead several days, already laid to rest in his tomb, when Jesus arrived on the scene. After the tomb was opened, Jesus prayed and then called out in a loud voice, "Lazarus come out!" (John 11:43), and Lazarus did! However, he must have been having difficulty walking since his hands and feet were wrapped with strips of linen and his face was covered by a cloth. Jesus turned to the family members and onlookers standing there and instructed them: "Take off the grave clothes and let him go" (John 11:44).

Lazarus, come out—Take off the grave clothes and let him go. There are two profound realities here. Jesus commanded Lazarus to come out, and out he came. He regained his life, something only Jesus could do, but he still needed help removing the grave clothes so he could move, walk, and get back to the business of living. Jesus instructed the onlookers to get involved.

I think that there is a lesson here for all of us. As I pointed out earlier in this chapter, we are not Jesus. Jesus is the one who restores life and raises all of us from the dead, out of the ditch, if you will, but we do have an important part to play. Our role is to assist in the process of healing by loosening the bindings that hold others back. Our job is to help suffering souls to get back on their feet, to take a few first cautious steps, and to eventually journey on down the road. This story reminds us of the important role we play in the lives of others, and it also serves as a reminder that when we ask God to make us the cup of strength to suffering souls, we do so in the name of Jesus.

Some Practical Advice

Since this chapter offers a succession of practical advice, I will only briefly review several pointers here to serve as a summary for those of us who truly desire to serve others in helpful and hopeful ways. First, embrace the reality that we cannot help everyone. That is not our calling. There are actually two pieces of good new here. The first is that there is a God. That is the indispensable reality from which we minister to others. The second is equally important—we are not God. Our calling begins with the earnest prayer that God will make us the cup of strength to a few suffering souls. We do not do this work on our own. In fact, we cannot.

The second bit of practical advice is to avoid trying to be the hero, swooping in to make everything all right or the difficulties simply go away. Our job is to help others out of the ditch and walk with them on down the road; it is not to become their parent or to save the circus. It is important to keep the focus on the situation and on God's grace and healing. It is not about us.

A third word of advice is to avoid taking on other's pain, suffering, and anger as your own. It really will not help them, but it will hurt you—and hinder your ministry. It is important to recognize and empathize with someone's feelings when they are in the ditch. It is another thing altogether to jump into the ditch with them. It is important to exercise restraint and self-care.

Finally, be patient. Others will not always respond in the way we would or did in a similar situation, or on our particular time frame. Healing takes time, and the clock is different for each one of us. Let the healing process work, walk alongside, be a friend, and let God do the heavy lifting.

Conclusion

As we near the conclusion of this prayer, we look back of what an incredible journey it has been for each of us—from a desperate cry for help from God for enough strength to get through the day without losing faith or hope—to the desire to share our deep joy and gladness and our journey with other suffering souls. After all, we have been in the ditch, too, and have some wisdom to share. We affirm a profound calling to recognize and minister to others in their time of need, to give something back, and to share the fathomless grace of God with anyone who will listen.

We recognized, however, that there can be some pitfalls when we reach out to others who are in the ditches of life. It is easy to get trapped in the mind-set that we must save everyone, the entire world. Honestly that cannot be done, and thankfully we are not called to that task. We have to let God be God. And it is important to avoid the real temptation to jump into situations and try to save the entire circus. We can serve as a Sherpa who guides the way and walks with others, but everyone has to carry their own pack up the mountain. And it is crucial to practice self-care, to avoid taking on the emotions accompanying others' troubles and difficulties. When we join in the emotional festivities, we do not help the one in the ditch, and may end up in the ditch ourselves.

It is truly an act of grace to be able to share the insights and faith we have gained from our own experiences in the ditch, even those of our own doing, with other suffering souls. Truly, we have some hard-earned wisdom to share, and it starts with the honesty to say, "Me, too," and the humility to listen rather than turn into a spouting fountain of unwanted advice. In compassion and community, grace has come full circle. It is both a mystery and a miracle, and at the end of the day, we can all say *thank you*! We join the multitudes who have sung over the centuries, "God is our refuge and strength, an ever-present help in trouble" (Ps 46:1). May it always be so in our lives, and in the lives of those we seek to serve.

Questions for Reflection and Discussion

1. Think back on a very difficult time in your life. In some way, did you or someone close to you go through the grieving process? How long did it take for healing and perspective to come?

2. Are you more inclined to try to save the entire world (take on every suffering soul) or to jump in and try to make everything alright (save the circus) when someone is in the ditch? Why is that so?

3. When you walk with someone who has been hurt, are you susceptible to taking on and carrying their hurt and anger? How can you be a supportive friend without getting stuck in the ditch, too?

4. In many supportive roles, it is easy to get a bit impatient with someone who is not "moving on" as easily or quickly as you would like or think they should. That is actually a natural reaction, but what tempering strategies can you use to give space and time for someone to heal at their own pace?

5. While ministering to others, what are the most effective and essential self-care practices for you? What fills your spiritual cup so that you can serve out of the overflow of your own spiritual life? Are you intentional about self-care? If not, what would be a good starting point?

FOR TODAY

O God:
Give me strength to live another day;
Let me not turn coward before its difficulties or prove recreant to its duties;
Let me not lose faith in other people;
Keep me sweet and sound of heart, in spite of ingratitude, treachery, or meanness;
Preserve me from minding little stings or giving them;
Help me to keep my heart clean, and to live so honestly and fearlessly that no outward failure can dishearten me or take away the joy of conscious integrity;
Open wide the eyes of my soul that I may see good in all things;
Grant me this day some new vision of thy truth;
Inspire me with the spirit of joy and gladness; and make me the cup of strength to suffering souls . . .

Closing Comments

The first question which the priest and the Levite asked was: "If I stop to help this man, what will happen to me?" But . . . the good Samaritan reversed the question: "If I do not stop to help this man, what will happen to him?"

—MARTIN LUTHER KING JR.

The Story of the Good Samaritan

The story of the Good Samaritan is one of the most familiar of all of Jesus' parables (Luke 10:25–37). I think it is so because all of us can find ourselves in the story and identify with one of the characters—and usually two or three at some point or another in our own spiritual journey. As you may recall, an expert in the law stood up and asked Jesus how he might inherit eternal life. Jesus turned the question around, asking the teacher what he thought. "Love the Lord with all your heart and with all your soul and with all your strength and with all your mind, and, Love your neighbor as yourself" (v. 27) was his instant response, and Jesus affirmed that he had answered correctly. All the teacher had to do, it followed, was to live it out, making it a reality in his own life.

But not quite ready to concede the point, the teacher pushed back and asked, "And who is my neighbor?" (v. 29) to which Jesus simply told this story: It seems a man was traveling the road from Jerusalem to Jericho when he was attacked, beaten, stripped naked, robbed, and left half-dead by the side of the road, literally in the ditch. A priest, and then a Levite, saw him, but passed by on the other side of the road. They were too busy or too afraid or too righteous to help out. Then a Samaritan came by. (Remember that the Jews and Samaritans were bitter enemies, and the Jews would have nothing to do with Samaritans.) Despite this reality, the Samaritan took pity on the man in the ditch, treated his wounds, took him to an inn, and paid for his care for the duration of his recovery.

At the conclusion of the story, Jesus turned once again to the teacher of the law and asked him who was "the neighbor" in the story. The teacher pointed out the man who showed mercy, and Jesus said, "Go and do likewise" (v. 37). I am sure this admonition was meant for more than just the teacher of the law; in fact, I believe that he was speaking to all of us. As a way of concluding our work together, let's see how this parable relates to "For Today," the prayer that we have been examining together in this book.

The One in the Ditch

At one time or another, we all end up in the ditch. We start out the day heading down the road from Jerusalem to Jericho, but we do not make it home by dark. Instead, we end up on the side of the road—beaten, robbed, naked, and afraid—ambushed by unexpected circumstances, sometimes the result of our own poor choices. And our pain is multiplied by the isolation and loneliness we feel as we watch others pass by on the other side of the road, unwilling or unable to even acknowledge us, let alone lend a helping hand.

We cry out to God, asking for strength to make it through the day without losing faith in others or the courage to squarely face our difficulties. We also pray for a clean heart and to be kept from minding or giving little stings in the face of ingratitude, treachery, and meanness. Above all else, we pray for a new vision of God's truth, the ability to see good in all the things we experience, even in the awful circumstances we face. But we are a long way from home, and we know that we need help—today.

What we need now, more than anything else, is someone who will see us, stop, and take pity on us, and get us off the side of the road and to an inn. We need someone who will assure us that better days are ahead, although it will take time. We need someone who will walk with us today and care for our immediate needs. Someone who can testify that God will set a table for us in the midst of our enemies, bidding us to come and dine, offering healing, hope, and grace—because that is what God does. We are in desperate need of spiritual and emotional triage from someone—anyone, a stranger, even a Samaritan. Hopefully, we can be the cup of strength to someone someday, but not this day. Today, the cup is empty and we are the one in need, stuck in the ditch by the side of the road.

The Samaritan

Sometimes we are called or summoned to be the Samaritan—a first responder of sorts to someone who is in the ditch. We are called to offer immediate support, insight, encouragement, and first aid. We are summoned to be a cup of strength to another suffering soul without yielding to the temptation to walk by, or to jump in—taking control of the entire situation, or attempting to make all the problems simply go away. No, our ministry is to give some immediate aid and comfort, to just show up, and to get the suffering soul to an inn. It may cost us some of our own time and resources, but it is one of the most significant roles we will ever play—even if we do not know the person we are assisting.

The Innkeeper

Sometimes we have the opportunity to be the caregiver, helping to nurse wounded souls back to spiritual health, walking with them on the long road to recovery. Note that the innkeeper did not ask for this role; he was in the business of renting out rooms. But when the Samaritan arrived with a badly beaten stranger, the innkeeper added to his daily routine—tending wounds, changing bandages, and providing sustenance, care, and encouragement during the recovery. He was literally the cup of strength to that suffering soul.

When we serve others, we do so with a spirit of joy and gladness that is nourished by a deep contentment that easters up within us when we look back on our own spiritual journeys, seeing God's fingerprints all over the place. We simply say, "Me, too," and we draw courage, perspective, and faith from God's faithfulness, and it is from this overflow that we can be the cup of strength to other suffering souls.

The Priest, the Levite, or the Samaritan?

Perhaps the most compelling question posed by this story is this: when we see someone in the ditch, what part will we play? Will we be like the priest, too busy dealing with our own church obligations to get involved in the mess? Or will we be like the Levite, so concerned about looking respectable, keeping clean, and following the rules that compassion and care do not fit in our daily schedule? Or will we be the one who knows from firsthand experience that we serve a God who came running to us while we were still a long way off, welcoming us home and celebrating our return, and we feel summoned to do the same? Will we stop by the side of the road because we serve a God who asks us to love our neighbors with everything we have, even neighbors we do not know—or even like?

Priest, Levite, or Samaritan—the choice is ours. May we always be mindful that we were once in the ditch, too, and whatever we offer in service to others, we do so in the name of the strong Deliverer, our only Lord and Savior, Jesus Christ. My sincere desire for each of us is that this prayer, "For Today," will find a significant place in your own spiritual practices, serving as a daily reminder that while life is messy, God is faithful.

And may we be found faithful, too, loving God with everything we have—heart, soul, mind, and strength, and our neighbors as ourselves—as if life together depended on it. The longer I journey, the more I am convinced that it does, wherever we find ourselves in the story—Samaritan, innkeeper, or the one left in the ditch by the side of the road. At the end of the day, we really do need each other, and together we can get home before dark.

FOR TODAY

O God:
Give me strength to live another day;
Let me not turn coward before its difficulties or prove recreant to its duties;
Let me not lose faith in other people;
Keep me sweet and sound of heart, in spite of ingratitude, treachery, or meanness;
Preserve me from minding little stings or giving them;
Help me to keep my heart clean, and to live so honestly and fearlessly that no outward failure can dishearten me or take away the joy of conscious integrity;
Open wide the eyes of my soul that I may see good in all things;
Grant me this day some new vision of thy truth;
Inspire me with the spirit of joy and gladness;
And make me the cup of strength to suffering souls;
In the name of the strong Deliverer, our only Lord and Savior, Jesus Christ.
—*PHILLIPS BROOKS*

www.ingramcontent.com/pod-product-compliance
Lightning Source LLC
Chambersburg PA
CBHW031427150426
43191CB00006B/433